M000199344

The Empath Self-Care Blueprint:

How to Manage, Navigate, and Thrive in an Overwhelming World

by Nick Trenton

www.NickTrenton.com

Table of Contents

Chapter One. Diagnosing the Empath

Maybe people constantly tell you to grow a thicker skin or to "stop being so sensitive."

Maybe you've noticed how easily a negative person can completely throw your mood.

Maybe you avoid the news or scary movies because it's as though you *literally* experience the fear of people on-screen.

If you're like many "sensitive" or feeling oriented people, you may have stumbled on the label of *empath* and immediately felt validated—could being finely tuned to the emotions of others, slightly introverted, or complex emotionally be not only normal but even a good thing?

The world is quickly becoming enamored with what used to be a niche topic; today, empaths are speaking out, forming support groups, writing books, and sharing experiences online. More and more people are stepping up and claiming this—not to mention enterprising individuals now positioning themselves to offer expensive training courses, healing sessions, and self-help packages to sell to the growing number of people callings themselves empaths.

Spend any time researching this topic online, and you may quickly get confused. Some empaths treat their personalities almost as an enviable superpower, while others act as though their abilities are a terrible weakness that means they need to "shield" from others. Some empaths lump their characteristics with ESP or even psychic powers, like predicting the future. Others claim an intense bond with nature.

Some frame their experiences in relational terms, and point to the perils of getting involved with "energy vampires" and narcissists who would seek to take advantage of their emotional intelligence and generosity. On the other hand, critics of the entire concept have suggested that the label is pure fiction, and one that introverted people with mental health disorders are drawn to.

As the conversation around the special type of person we call an "empath" grows, more and more is seemingly added to the definition. You could be forgiven for asking, what is an empath *really*? And more importantly, are you one?

Let's begin by trimming down to the basics on which everyone can agree—an empath is a person with a heightened capacity for empathy, or someone with the ability to feel the emotions of others.

Rather than merely understanding another person's state of mind on an *intellectual* level, empaths seem to "let more in," and can find themselves literally feeling the emotional reality of another person. This is a psychological definition rather than a spiritual or esoteric one, although it's easy to imagine that the lines blur. Many empaths additionally describe themselves as extrasensory and intensely interested in psychic phenomena, spiritual matters, or learning to sense the emotions of even animal or extraterrestrial "energies."

We can understand empaths as supremely *emotionally intelligent* in the way that some people are gifted with musical ability, or are born with heightened taste buds and become acclaimed chefs. An empath could be seen as more emotionally aware or more sensitive to emotional stimuli than the average person. Like an animal that can see in ultraviolet light or hear super high frequency sounds, an empath seems to inhabit a different world entirely—one dominated by *felt experience*, i.e. emotion.

Empaths have been described as excellent listeners and truly compassionate, generous people. Others describe their enormous ability to care about others; they're gentle, perceptive and insightful people with a natural flair for understanding others— sometimes even better than they do themselves.

On the other hand, it's this very ability to allow in the emotions of others that can overwhelm an empath, deplete them, or have them unable to discern whose feelings are whose! An empath without an understanding of their unique characteristics can quickly find themselves retreating from the world to "recover," or worse, falling into relationships with people who would actively exploit and manipulate them, even as they try valiantly to "rescue" them. Yes, empaths can also be easily targeted by certain types of people because of their willingness to engage and feel.

Emotions are sadly afforded little attention or respect in our world today, a world that surely isn't built for such an immersive experience. An empath can feel like they're an alien in a foreign world, perceiving and being affected by things other people don't comprehend. It's understandable that people who identify primarily as emotional and empathic beings are happy to discover a term that describes their unique strengths not as a failure, but simply as another way of being.

Many empaths have struggled for years before having the courage to reframe their experiences and reclaim their unique ability to *feel* in a world that strongly discourages it. Putting a name to this term, and simply having the knowledge that they are far from alone, can be empowering and comforting.

But simply having a name for this special kind of person is not enough. If you identify as an empath, the question is, *what next?* Well, because we have a label, we can dictate a path for better living and taking advantage of this trait rather than falling victim to it. At first, we will be left with more questions than answers, but we will slowly work our way through the following in this book:

- Is being an empath an inborn skill or something you can learn?
- How is life different for an empath, and what does it mean to consider yourself one?
- How do empaths get to be the way they are?
- Are empaths really better than everyone else—more spiritually enlightened, kinder and so on?
- What makes an empath happy and healthy?

- What does an unhealthy empath look like? Do empaths suffer from anxiety and depression more?
- Is being an empath the same as being a Highly Sensitive Person (HSP) or an introvert, or something completely different?
- Does being an empath affect your career and your relationships, and if so, how?

Ultimately, what an empath is can vary widely depending on who you ask! In the chapters of this book we'll consider all the many facets of being an empath to help you decide for yourself if identifying this way resonates with you. We'll look at ways to decide if you are an empath, learn skills to enhance your strengths and mitigate your weaknesses, and learn how to communicate your needs and experiences to other people. We'll take a look at some aspects of the discussion that are a little more controversial, and answer the above question and more. The first question we'll look at is the obvious one—are *you* an empath?

Why do I feel so intensely?

The first thing to understand is that being an empath is a relatively new idea, and there are no fixed, standardized definitions available (yet?). Though people throughout history have had different ways of talking about sensitive, delicate, ultra-compassionate or perceptive people, the term "empath" is only a few years old, and most are unfamiliar with the term. It's not a "diagnosis," psychiatric or otherwise, and many people simply decide that if the description fits, then they are happy to think of themselves as empaths.

That said, more and more mental health experts are weighing in on the idea, with the most prominent perhaps being Dr. Judith Orloff, an American psychiatrist who wrote the influential book *The Empath's Survival Guide* in 2017. Since then, content has sprung up everywhere to talk about what an empath is, how to identify them, and how to "survive." Even neurosurgeons have been investigating the claims of empaths to determine whether they actually differ in the way their brains function. There are a few real biological differences between the brains of introverts and extroverts, so it may not be surprising that the brain of the empathetic is different as well.

What follows is a list of traits, experiences, beliefs, feelings, capacities, and idiosyncrasies that seem common to most empaths, but it's important to remember one thing: these lists are not definitive in any sense, and there is no special secret club of empaths who will only admit you if you tick enough boxes! Rather, these descriptions are offered to help put a finger on some of the more subtle experiences that strongly emotional and sensitive people experience. The idea is not to get bogged down in who is and who is not a "real" empath, but to navigate our own identities with care and compassion. Rather than seeing how high we can score, we can use these lists to learn more about ourselves and what we need for our wellbeing.

The list Orloff gives is as follows:

- Have I been labeled as "too emotional" or overly sensitive?
- If a friend is distraught, do I start feeling it too?
- Are my feelings easily hurt?
- Am I emotionally drained by crowds, require time alone to revive?
- Do my nerves get jarred by noise, smells, or excessive talk?
- Do I prefer taking my own car places so that I can leave when I please?
- Do I overeat to cope with emotional stress?
- Am I afraid of becoming engulfed by intimate relationships?

If you answer "yes" to one to three of these questions, you're at least part empath, but responding to more than three is a strong indication that you're an empath. Other people have given slightly different lists, claiming that empaths are:

- Sensitive, big-hearted, tender, nurturing.
- Able to absorb the emotions of others, and feeling like other people's

negative emotions can overwhelm them.

- Often introverts, since crowds and big groups can feel draining. They may choose to regularly recharge their batteries with alone time—or risk exhaustion if they ignore their need to retreat.
- Deeply intuitive, and can "sense" even subtle shifts in mood, pick up on concealed emotions, tell when people are lying, or even understand someone's innermost experience within minutes of meeting them. An empath who follows their gut is seldom wrong!
- Overwhelmed in crowded or busy places.
- Nature lovers. Many empaths feel rejuvenated and balanced in nature, near the ocean, forests, or animals. Empaths seldom feel happy in bustling cityscapes, malls, or traffic.
- Literally sensitive, in that their senses are often heightened. They may notice changes in smells, sounds, textures on their skin, light levels,

etc., and be deeply affected by these where others might not even notice.

- Sometimes guilty of having poor boundaries. These are the people who cannot see suffering without trying to help in some way. This can leave them exhausted, cynical, and run down, however.
- Often find that people gravitate toward them and want to share their deepest secrets and problems.
- Easily targeted by individuals who have relatively less empathy, i.e. narcissistic individuals or those who want to exploit an empath's kindness. Empaths can unwittingly become involved in toxic relationships with others to their own detriment.
- Deeply affected by depressing news, violence on TV, or the stories of other people's suffering.
- Often overwhelmed in close, intimate relationships. Ironically, deep intimacy can be threatening for someone who feels as deeply as an empath does. Romantic relationships can sometimes lead an empath to

feeling overwhelmed, or as though they "lose themselves."

- Often drawn to caring professions.
- Often able to physically feel emotions, such as feeling sick and unwell around angry people.
- Unable to say no as often as they'd like, and may constantly be drawn to being the helper or rescuer.
- Unable to tolerate much conflict. Empaths try hard to create harmony and cohesion, and can find disharmony very upsetting, often finding themselves the peacemakers.
- Able to tell when people are being insincere.
- Able to almost predict what will happen next because of how deeply they understand the present emotional situation.
- Sometimes alienated, feeling as though they're very different from others, and alone in the way they see the world. Empaths can feel very passionately about topics others don't understand, and this can leave them feeling abnormal or outcast.

If you're an empath, you've likely been told in life that you're too sensitive, too intense, a "big softie," an idealist, very perceptive, kind and compassionate, or even a bit of a doormat! Though the above are the most commonly accepted traits of being an empath, others have shared unique experiences that may resonate with you: perhaps you have a problem with emotional eating, or suffer with energy levels or tricky illnesses like IBS, chronic fatigue or migraines—signs that you're holding on to emotions in your body. Perhaps you have issues with depression and anxiety. Many empaths are vegan or vegetarian or passionately involved in campaigning for justice and equal rights.

Others have suggested that empaths are not just able to pick up other people's emotions, but can "tune in" to the world at large, and many report feeling positively overcome with grief when contemplating environmental degradation. An empath may identify so much with being a caring, giving person that they quickly become martyrs in their own lives, losing touch with the ability to care for themselves or identify their own wants and needs in a sea of other peoples'.

Empaths can be spiritually gifted, artistic, or unique in many other ways, but they don't have to be—they come from all walks of life, and the only thing they seem to routinely have in common is a heightened capacity for emotional empathy for others. If you can confidently say that you feel that you do this more than the average person, it's likely you're an empath. Let's delve a little deeper.

Origins, Causes, and Journeys

If you're like most people who eventually come to call themselves empaths, you may have felt this way your entire life. Many empaths describe knowing that they were different from a very young age, and having troubled childhoods as they grappled with the intense and often overwhelming burden of feeling as much as they do.

But does this mean that a "normal" person is lacking something in comparison to an empath? Surely every human would like to believe that they are caring, considerate, and empathetic? There are countless well-adjusted, caring, and happy people in the world who would nevertheless *not* identify as empaths. And yet there is still a marked and obvious difference when trying to compare life experiences.

What can this tell us about the life path of the empath and how they arrive at their unique set of abilities?

Let's examine all the factors that make empaths what they are. There are several models and theories that try to understand the development of the empathic personality, but most of them fall in roughly four categories: genetics (i.e. empaths inherit the trait from their parents), inborn temperament or character (i.e. from birth), the result of childhood trauma, or, on the other hand, the result of positive parenting that helps those with inborn gifts to develop them properly.

The way that people (and empaths themselves) talk about the cause and history of their unique set of characteristics has important consequences—for example, some empaths see their abilities as something they control and can be proud of, but others believe that who they are is an unavoidable result of trauma, neglect, or abuse in childhood, and they spend considerable efforts to "fix" themselves or overcome what they perceive as a weakness.

The reality is likely to be somewhere in between. Consider how we think about other traits that we have—we may not be able to change them completely, but we can certainly learn to use them in more productive and empowering ways to the point that it can become a huge strength. The first step to this process is an awareness that something needs to change, and if you're reading this sentence, you're already far past this point.

Whichever way a person chooses to think about empaths, one thing is consistent: these are people who do not react to external stimuli in a "normal" way. Whether because of an innate characteristic, or because of parenting that has worn down certain natural barriers and boundaries, empaths seem to have a lower threshold for emotional arousal, and can be thrown off balance by stimuli that would not bother another person. Again, it's no different from having a certain sensitivity to taste, sense, smell, touch, or bright colors—any of the normal five senses.

For ongoing growth and comfort, it's important that empaths find others like them, and especially seek out help and support from professionals who not only understand the empath phenomenon but think about it in the same way as the empath themselves. Much of the early writing—including Orloff's book—focuses on the narrative of the empath as a fragile, delicate person who needs to "heal" and find ways to protect themselves in a big, brash world.

However, other empath writers have argued that this is an essentially disempowering narrative and that if empaths are truly to own and accept who they are, they need to stop talking about their personalities as though they were disabilities, or something akin to an allergy or intolerance. Rather, many empaths have found their journeys have taken them on other paths—i.e. ones where they think of their empathic abilities more as a muscle to be trained and flexed, or a tool that simply needs to be understood to be used wisely. That's certainly the approach that I want to take—arming you with tools and techniques to harness your abilities into a superpower.

While it's true that empaths can become exhausted and unwell by constantly internalizing the emotional state of others, they can learn to moderate these effects and use their empathy more consciously, directing it at will and learning how to use healthy boundaries so they can be *more* compassionate and sensitive, not less.

What does the science say?

There have now been many studies done directly in empathy, but also in the field of compassion, neurotransmitters like dopamine, and how emotions really work in the body. The so-called "mirror neuron system" is a clump of brain cells strongly associated with compassion, i.e. the ability to "mirror" another person's emotions. They literally provide the ability to see and understand someone. Some research has suggested that empaths have stronger, more, or better-wired mirror neurons, while people with narcissistic personality disorder may lack this ability, and hence have difficulty empathizing with others.

These same mirror neurons help empaths create a "neuro-physical" link between themselves and others so that the areas stimulated in their brains by *someone else's* emotion is the same as if it had occurred to *them*. This is a powerful idea and explains why empaths feel others so strongly—as strongly as other people feel their own emotions! This degree of "neural resonance" has been shown to vary in people, however, and super empathetic people might be that way because of their overactive mirror-neuron system.

Another idea is that of "emotional contagion" which is not unique to empaths but could go some way to explaining why some people can "catch" emotions more than others. All humans are social animals who respond to the emotions of those around us, even to the point of unconsciously mimicking them.

For instance, think about how suddenly intense and aroused you may become if you are in the middle of a crowd at a sporting event. It may be a far cry from your normal personality, but you've just been infected, so to speak. Research in this area has shown how often people synchronize their emotions in group settings—one crying baby will often set off another, or one depressed person in the office will soon have everyone feeling depressed. Your friend yawns, and you do too.

Emotional contagion can happen with anyone, but our unique personalities may mean that we're more likely to be either "senders" or "catchers" in the energy dynamic that happens when two people encounter one another. The catcher is more powerfully drawn to the emotional state of the sender, who dominates or catches others in their "orbit" and is often a charismatic, entertaining, or even domineering person. In this model, influential or powerful people set the emotional tone, and others follow, like how a boss or parental figure can change the entire mood of the home or office.

Subsequent research has seen people try to deny that empathy is merely emotional contagion. These researchers claim that while emotional contagion is quick, unsophisticated, and largely unconscious, true empathy is more about genuinely considering and understanding the perspective of another person.

They believe that merely soaking up others' emotions is not really what healthy empathy is about, and many of the negative traits associated with empaths come from this inability to self-regulate or maintain appropriate boundaries. Furthermore, this model doesn't explain *why* empaths would experience this to a greater degree than others, but it does highlight that empathy falls on a spectrum, with some individuals showing higher sensitivity than others.

A less well-known idea is that electromagnetic fields are generated by the heart and the brain, and that these can transmit emotional information between people—a process that empaths are particularly sensitive to. Unfortunately, not only does this not really explain why empaths are more sensitive to these fields than others, but the model is largely considered pseudoscience, and there is no evidence to support the idea that this is how emotions, or empathy, work.

A more promising theory is that empaths have different hormonal and neurotransmitter regulation, resulting in them having a higher sensitivity to dopamine. This means introverted empaths need less stimulation to feel happy and content, and can feel strong wellbeing from simply staying at home, reading or meditating, compared to extroverts, who need larger doses of dopamine, such as in big crowds or exciting events.

Again, though there is some evidence to suggest that people display different sensitivities to dopamine, this trait interacts with many others and can be altered by drugs or certain behaviors, such as exercise. Though empaths may well have different biochemistry when compared to non-empaths, there is probably a lot more to the empath story than neurotransmitters, not to mention the question of why empaths differ in the first place!

A final strand of research is trying to connect the phenomenon of "mirror touch synesthesia" (MTS) with empathy. MTS is a neurological condition that results in the perception of two separate senses being combined in the brain—for example, tasting music, hearing colors, or seeing shapes when you touch different textures. Some people with synesthesia can watch another person get touched and feel the touch on their own bodies. Judith Orloff believes that empaths may be a form of mirror touch synesthesia, i.e. feeling the emotions of others in one's own body *as if it was one's own*. In other words, the empath channels the perception of external emotions through their own, and experiences unrelated stimuli as part of their own inner world.

Let's consider the psychological or developmental theories, i.e. the idea that childhood experiences determine whether a person becomes an empath. From the psychoanalytic perspective, an "ego boundary" is the line we all must draw between ourselves and others. It's not something we are born with—in fact, we are born with the opposite, where our concept of ourselves is necessarily combined with that of others.

In infancy, this boundary is not yet solid—when we are born, we scarcely think of ourselves as an ego at all, and may wholly identify with our mothers, or simply believe that we are all that exists in the world, unable yet to imagine that other people exist with different inner worlds than ours. We are simply not independent beings until much later in life, and that's a process of normal psychological development.

Because infants depend on adults for survival, they soon learn to "read" those around them and behave as they do, even mirroring their emotions while their own are still relatively undeveloped. Children who have been abused or had narcissistic or negligent parents may have become extra talented at detecting the tiniest expressions or changes in mood so that they could pre-empt an attack or abandonment. This is where the psychological development may take a detour.

In this model, empathic abilities arise out of a need to protect the self, but in the process, the ego boundary becomes too permeable, leaving the adult with a constant sense of overwhelm, of being too sensitive, and of feeling like they could "lose themselves." This is the model of behavior that worked and protected them the best during their upbringing, but it may not serve a real purpose anymore. Empaths are thus seen to be traumatized and hypervigilant rather than strictly intuitive, and have learnt to scan the tiniest details of their emotional environment because of difficult childhoods.

If a child constantly has their boundaries violated or ignored, they may soon lose the ability to self-regulate and monitor these boundaries. A parent who is overly demanding, violates privacy, or holds the child responsible for the parent's emotions may create an adult who cannot successfully draw a line around themselves. They may feel invaded by the demands and emotions of others—on the one hand strongly identifying with the caring, even savior role, but quickly getting depleted and overcome by it all.

Some empaths find themselves "enmeshed" with their caregivers who are unable to let them grow out of their initial infant dependency on them. A parent who makes a child feel guilty for leaving them, and one way or another encroaches their own needs and emotions too far into the child's world, will create an adult who feels burdened by obligation and duty.

Boundaries are blurred, and one person's emotions spill over into another. A child growing up in such a household is said to not have the opportunity to develop healthy boundaries, and may go on to have traits described as heightened "empathy." As adults, they may have a hard time deciding which are their emotions and which rightly belong to others, or else they may constantly find themselves drawn into codependent scenarios where they struggle pointlessly to rescue someone else from their own negative emotions. Again, this may have served them at some point in their lives, but in most instances, this is likely hurting you more than benefiting.

Many empaths will describe feeling used by others as an "emotional sponge" onto which thoughtless others can dump unwanted negative emotion. This is where the narrative about "energy vampires" come in, although in reality, the dynamic is probably held in place by both parties. The psychoanalytic concept of *projection* can help us understand this a little.

When we project, we are disowning unwanted and unacknowledged parts of our own psyche onto others in order to avoid seeing it in ourselves. Empaths with poorer ego boundaries will find themselves the target of projection more often than others, the theory goes. What's worse, they may receive the projection of someone else *and identify with it*, unable to see that it doesn't really belong to them or even behave in ways that confirm the projection.

For example, a person may be highly motivated to achieve and succeed, but feel unable to acknowledge a part of his personality that feels weak, vulnerable, and ashamed. In a conversation with an empath, such a person may unconsciously project this shame and vulnerability onto the empath, and make them feel like they are inferior, a failure, and so on. The empath may in turn accept all this without even realizing that the source of these feelings is external. They may feel exhausted after the exchange without knowing why. If this was something that happened regularly, you can understand why an empath would prefer to stay at home and avoid it all!

The Double-Edged Sword

Most empaths feel that their unique blend of characteristics is both a blessing and a drawback, a gift and a curse. On some days, they may feel proud of their totally different, often beautiful and rich perspective on the world, and on other days, it can feel like a burden and something to carefully manage in a world that doesn't properly cater to them. It really comes down to awareness and harnessing this ability rather than letting it run roughshod all over your life.

Thankfully, more and more people are appreciating just how valuable empaths are as employees, friends, family members, business leaders, and more. The message is loud and clear: the world needs empaths! There is a growing amount of external validation and recognition for such abilities and mindsets.

Empowered empaths can be incredibly powerful and inspiring individuals, with a capacity to experience a vision of the world that is profound and beautiful. When healthy, they can lead with charisma and gravity, promoting harmony and balance in a world that sorely lacks both. When an empath is tuned into their emotions and practices discernment, they can be extraordinary individuals, capable of feats of intuition that may even seem supernatural or mystical.

A healthy empath is often on an intense inner journey that enlivens and enriches everyone they encounter. Able to absorb, process, and integrate enormous volumes of emotional material, an empath can be a powerful hub of healing and transformation. A strong empath is like a machine for generating love, meaning, and evolution. It's no surprise that some empaths find solace in developing their psychic abilities, flexing their ability to "read" energies, listening to their guts, and trusting larger forces in the universe that they feel uniquely plugged into. They are an irreplaceable part of every organization or family unit—this is always the role that someone needs to fill, for better or worse.

An empath can use their abilities to create real presence, dissolving fear and inviting others to be in the moment, in their bodies, and in their emotions. By bringing our own light to others, we can encourage them to get more familiar with their own emotions, accept their vulnerabilities and be open to change and growth. It's all this that makes empaths identify as healers—of the body, heart, and mind.

Empaths can channel extraordinary creativity, be phenomenal parents, and head projects and movements that seem to have an otherworldly quality. When empaths can fully own their abilities, they end up demonstrating an extraordinary strength and resilience—the courage to be gentle, to open instead of close, to choose love instead of fear.

Empaths, when they trust themselves, *know* things. They can pick up on "vibes," are open-minded, compassionate, and able to creatively put together rich and wonderful lives that are uniquely their own. It's no exaggeration to say that empaths are increasingly well situated for the future, where connectivity, creativity, and emotional intelligence will be even more sought after and valued. Empaths bring *heart* to the equation, and the world has been missing this ingredient for a long time. Socially minded, unselfish, responsible, cooperative, open-minded, and unconventional, business needs empaths to lead, inspire, and forge completely new paths into the future.

There is simply no area of life where increased emotional awareness, respect for others, and a heightened capacity for awareness are not advantageous. Their empathy and vision glues the world back together, rather than tears it apart; their strong moral compass and commitment to justice and fairness make them an asset wherever they find themselves, where their passion, generosity, and innovative way of looking at things only enriches the world around them.

The caveat, of course, is that all of this belongs to a healthy, actualized empath who not only knows and accepts their gifts but knows how to use them, despite or even because of early traumas and unhealed wounds. With proper boundaries, rock-solid self-respect, and a willingness to live quite differently from others, empaths can reach their full potential—and it's a lot of potential, indeed.

But what if empaths *aren't* empowered and strong and healed?

If we think of the empathic mind and heart as amplifiers, we can see how all the troubles of the world can get trapped and exaggerated, resulting in a person who experiences depths of pain and suffering that may go well beyond the "normal." Whether it's because they feel "too much," or take on the weight of the world's negative emotions, an out-of-balance or unhappy empath can rightly think of themselves as bearing a terrible curse.

Being so fine-tuned an instrument, an empath can get overwhelmed by the sheer force and negativity of other people's "stuff" coming their way. Bad moods, blame, shame, anger, and so on can affect you as much as a sick person could give you their flu. Empaths still learning about themselves may find that "they" are moody and shift constantly—but it's really that they've absorbed and internalized the emotions of others, which can leave them feeling untethered, volatile, and emotionally drained. Without proper awareness, an empath can simply feel like they can't fit anywhere into the world properly.

When this happens, an empath can be an unpleasant person. They can feel crabby, aloof, or antisocial, or get so irritable with others they can barely stand to socialize at all. They can start to feel that compassion is a terrible obligation, and get burnt out with the pain they feel in others and the world at large. If an empath is in a toxic or unhealthy relationship, they may find it difficult to ask for the vital alone time they need, resulting in them feeling even more worn out and even angry or cynical. An empath who isn't given the time to recuperate, integrate and heal themselves can even hurt others, become depressed or anxious, or feel generally crazy.

This imbalance and discomfort is not just emotional—an empath will feel it in their entire body, and may suffer sleeplessness, fatigue, mysterious aches and pains, weight gain, allergies or sensitivities, and a range of signals that they are badly out of whack. Empaths are kind, but they are not stupid— sadly, others will often take advantage of them, not appreciating the true value they offer and seeking instead to exploit them. People who are less able to process emotions may unconsciously hand over theirs to the empath for processing, and an empath who does this work for several people will soon find themselves with several peoples' worth of mental and physical trouble!

Emotions are sadly not honored or acknowledged for the powerful tools they are, and consequently, empaths, who could be masters of the emotional world, may feel isolated, undermined, ignored, or belittled by those who feel that toughness, ruthlessness, and machine-like efficiency are what makes a person worthwhile. An empath can feel like they're all alone in the world, unable to really communicate what they see or experience. They can feel like others are constantly testing their boundaries or taking advantage. A whole day can be ruined by a moment of violence on TV, a "small thing" that others brush off but which can leave them upset for days.

In short, being an empath is a double-edged sword. You feel *more*—more of the wonderful stuff, including profound love, connection, peace, the joy and essence of life flowing easily through you. But you also feel more of everything else, and are porous to hate, anger, closemindedness, and a host of negativity that comes from others. *An empath's success and wellbeing in life rests firmly in how well he or she can balance and negotiate these two forces.*

Takeaways

- What is an empath? Are you one? Why does the world appear so differently to you than to your friends? What is the cause of this, and what exactly is going on? You may very well be an empath. An empath is a person with a heightened capacity for empathy, or someone with the ability to feel the emotions of others.
- You feel *deeply*, and it's not a choice. Rather than merely understanding another person's state of mind on an *intellectual* level, empaths seem to "let more in, and can find themselves literally feeling the emotional reality of another person. We can understand empaths as supremely *emotionally intelligent* in the way that some people are gifted with musical ability or are born with heightened taste buds and become acclaimed chefs.

- There are several models and theories that try to understand the development of the empathic personality, but most of them fall in roughly four categories: genetics (i.e. empaths inherit the trait from their parents as a result of literally different brain chemistry in the form of mirror neurons and/or emotional contagion sensitivity), temperament or character (usually as a coping mechanism for self-protection, combined with a hazy understanding of personal boundaries), the result of childhood trauma (which for an empath can be something surprising) or, on the other hand, the result of positive parenting that helps those with inborn gifts to develop them properly.
- Most empaths feel that their unique blend of characteristics is both a blessing and a drawback; a gift and a curse. On some days, they may feel proud of their totally different, often beautiful and rich perspective on the world, and on other days, it can feel like a burden and something to carefully manage in a world that doesn't properly

cater to them. It really comes down to awareness and harnessing this ability rather than letting it run roughshod all over your life.

- There is simply no area of life where increased emotional awareness, respect for others, and a heightened capacity for awareness are not advantageous. But an empath who isn't given the time to recuperate, integrate, and heal themselves can even hurt others, become depressed or anxious, or feel generally crazy.

Chapter Two. Defining and Differentiating

We've taken a look at what an empath is, the signs you might be one, how you might have gotten to be that way (using scientific and not-so-scientific theories) and the underlying characteristics of all empaths, both good and bad. As we delve further, we need to also consider what it is that an empath *does*, i.e. what exactly empathy is— and what it isn't. Empaths surely have empathy, but it goes much deeper than that.

In the sections that follow, we'll compare the phenomenon of empathy with things it's often confused with, drawing a clearer definition around the unique characteristics of empaths. We'll also draw clear lines between different types of personality phenomenon to further our understanding. By the end of these first two chapters, you should have a lucid view of how the empath stands apart from just about everyone else in the world.

Exponential Empathy

Empathy is that human ability to see, comprehend, and share the emotions of another being, whether that's another person, a fictional character, an animal, or even something more abstract like plants or the earth itself. When we practice empathy, what we are doing is temporarily stepping outside of our point of view to try on another's—i.e. we don't see them as ourselves, but *see them as they see themselves* (this is a vital but often misunderstood difference between sympathy and empathy).

In a world where empathy is seemingly on the decline, the above description can seem wishy-washy or abstract, but there is plenty of neuroscientific research to back up the existence of empathy in the brain. What is it that makes you flinch when you see a character on TV get hurt? Some researchers are now finding that areas of the brain (the insula and anterior cingulate cortex) get activated *as though the event had happened to us firsthand.* Our own emotions and sensations are aroused when we witness someone else's emotions. This mirror system can help us make the imaginative leap to understand the world through someone else—a pretty big deal when you think about it.

Vicariously witnessing the state of mind of others can lead us to replicating it within ourselves, and this is perhaps the root of our "theory of mind"—our guess at what it's like to be someone other than ourselves. Psychopaths lack this ability and seem unable to feel another's pain, although there is some suggestion that they can learn to. This may also suggest that empathy falls on a scale, with people showing varying degrees that can be strengthened or downplayed at will. For instance, you might have more empathy toward a homeless person if they showed a remarkable resemblance to your parent, and you have might less empathy if you were to simply read about a homeless person on the internet.

Other experiments have shown that if people have their own pain reduced, they are sometimes less able to empathize with others—a link that may seem very obvious to empaths. It may be that our ability to understand the pain of others is first rooted in our own pain, and we represent others' suffering using the palette of our own experience. Without a proper understanding of the human experience, emotions will be limited.

Other experiments have elaborated on this—by manipulating an area of the brain related to egocentricity, the right supramarginal gyrus. Researchers seemed able to manipulate the self/other divide that seems so fluid in empaths, and also found that people often interpret other peoples' emotions through their own emotional states at the time. Continued research into this area is showing us that empathy is not a fixed trait so much as an emergent phenomenon that can change according to culture, past experience, current emotional states, trauma, training, and more.

Types of Empathy

Sometimes people can talk about "empathy" for quite a while before they realize they are using completely different definitions of the term. After all, there are many different ways to "put yourself in someone's shoes," so it follows that there are many components to empathizing with someone.

Cognitive empathy is the ability to take on the mental perspective of another person, allowing you to, for example, understand what another person doesn't know, or how they're thinking about a particular problem. You can see and understand their state of being in the same way a psychiatrist may be able to look at a person's behavior and correctly identify which mental illness they're displaying, or apply a psychoanalytic model to explain the behavior. This kind of empathy is still empathy, but will seldom resonate with those who identify as empaths.

Emotional empathy, however, is more to do with *feeling together* with someone else, not merely understanding their emotions on an intellectual level. As we've already seen, this ability has both pros and cons, and if a person is naturally gifted at emotional empathy, they may need to learn special self-care techniques to maintain proper boundaries and self-awareness (we'll explore this more in later chapters).

Somatic empathy is occasionally mentioned, and is the ability to physically feel another's bodily sensations on your own body—something often reported with twins or when witnessing someone else enduring a horrible physical injury.

Compassionate empathy is sometimes mentioned as a healthier attitude to take than purely emotional, cognitive, or somatic empathy. Compassion is a deep, real understanding of another's pain, but is more positively geared toward fixing the problem without getting overwhelmed in negative emotions. Cognitive empathy would allow you to see the logical details of a problem. Emotional empathy might have you feeling equally as sad and depressed about the problem. But compassionate empathy may go a step further to uplift or improve the situation, or else help the other person be with their emotions without getting flooded by them yourself.

Compassionate empathy is sometimes practiced by very skilled psychologists, and shows that merely being able to feel another's pain is not always enough—and can sometimes only multiply suffering. A well-developed empath can learn to find the balance between being cold and uncaring and being overly invested in the emotions of others. This middle path is genuine compassion.

Spiritual empathy is somewhat related, and can be understood as a healthier connection with another through a shared spiritual interconnectedness. Many empaths find immense clarity, satisfaction, and meaning from sublimating bleeding-heart emotional empathy for a more conscious form of spiritual empathy—they are then able to feel with another's *soul*, to share in their life's journey, but without getting sucked into life dynamics that are not strictly theirs.

At this point, you might have noticed that all this talk of empathy makes no specific mention of empaths as a group of people separate somehow in their ability to empathize. Isn't empathy something that all humans can do?

While it's true that empaths don't hold the monopoly on the ability to feel into another person's world, the truth is that it's a matter of *degree*. In the same way as we can think of certain people as being intellectually gifted and able to process more cognitively than an average person, we can imagine an empath as someone who simply has a higher capacity for the normal human behavior of empathy. We all possess different personality traits and characteristics—and empathy is one of them. Some individuals simply demonstrate higher levels of this characteristic. Judith Orloff explains that empaths don't experience anything "normal" people can't, but they do experience it far more *intensely*.

Ordinary empathy may be more sporadic and occasional for some people, but for an empath it's a more or less constant state of mind, and they may be far more sensitive to even subtle shifts in energy and mood, well before others have noticed them. This is simply like having a very well-tuned sense, just as some have brilliant eyesight or an incredibly fine-tuned sense of smell. While most people can smell and see, a few people have abilities in these areas that distinguish them from the norm.

HSPs, Introverts, Codependents, and More

We've already seen that beyond the simple definition of "having a lot of empathy," the category of empath is a broad and rather loosely defined one. It has to do with feeling intense emotion to the point of being negatively affected.

Sadly, many people disagree with one another about who is and is not allowed to consider themselves an empath, and there is some confusion about how other traits, like being a Highly Sensitive Person (HSP), an introvert, or even a psychic, play into things. Debate can get heated over certain controversial ideas, and people can get attached to their own pet theories and ideas, feeling threatened if others they don't consider real empaths join the conversation.

This book will take the position that empaths exist as completely distinct from many of the personality types or behavioral disorders that they're often misdiagnosed with. We'll take a look at what distinguishes empaths from these other groups, but with the caveat that *not* being an empath is not a bad thing, just as being one isn't a badge of honor. It may also be wise to accept that human experience is complex and nuanced, and that every person's journey will be slightly different. There's nothing to say that a person cannot be an empath, an introvert, or a Highly Sensitive Person *and* suffer from borderline personality disorder, if that is indeed the best way they find to narrate their experience. In this spirit, let's look at some phenomenon commonly associated with (but not identical to) being an empath. Again, we want to make sure to be as exact and specific as possible when we define ourselves, because that is how we will find the best path forward and upward.

Dr. Elaine Aron popularized the topic of Highly Sensitive People in her book. HSPs and empaths have overlapping characteristics but are not (according to Judith Orloff, at least) the same. The common characteristics include being easily stimulated and feeling sensitive to not only loud or busy social gatherings, but also light, texture, smell, etc., a proneness to feeling emotionally burnt out, a love for nature, a rich inner life, compassion, and needing alone time to recover. But empaths can be introverted or extroverted, whereas HSPs are almost always introverts. Put another way, the HSP can be said to be more fragile, while the empath can be said to be more intuitive.

Some believe that empaths are different in that they can actually sense subtler "energy" fields and patterns around them, even taking them into their own bodies, which is something an HSP won't do. In other words, the empath takes things a bit further on the spectrum, often including profound spiritual insights or intuition into the mix, whereas an HSP might not.

The difference is not so much in the characteristics, but the degree to which those characteristics are present. It's important, though, to note that there is no "hierarchy" and that many authors disagree completely over the existence of HSPs, of empaths, of both, or of the idea that one is significantly different from the other. There is as yet no research to prove much about either empaths or HSPs, so it's probably worth approaching these labels as just that: useful ways to talk about patterns of experience.

What about the ideas of introversion and extroversion, and how do they play out in relation to empathy? An empath may well be an introvert, but an introvert doesn't necessarily have to be an empath. After all, some people may retreat from social life because they are simply not interested in it, whereas an empath might need to periodically withdraw precisely because they become so engrossed and overwhelmed by being social with others. Though the end result is them seeking alone time, an empath and a non-empath introvert might do so for very different reasons.

It's important to note that many people fundamentally misunderstand introversion to begin with. The common conception of an introvert is someone who perhaps seems socially anxious, awkward, maladjusted, unconfident, misanthropic, or even nerdy.

The real difference between introverts and extroverts, however, is that the former can find social experiences draining rather than energizing, and will need to seek alone time to recover and "top up" before being social again, whereas the latter will find socializing itself very energizing, and will seek it out, finding themselves missing social contact. Introverts can love people, be charming, popular, and friendly, and sincerely enjoy socializing—they just do it at a different degree than extroverts, and will also savor alone time.

Now, an HSP may look like an introvert because their threshold for stimulation is very low. This means that a gathering of two close friends can *feel* as exhausting as a massive party to them. But the difference between empaths and HSPs is in the name—HSPs are simply sensitive. They are more affected by stimuli than others, like an instrument calibrated to detect even the tiniest changes. An empath, on the other hand, doesn't respond more to the same stimuli, but actually *feels others* as a stimulus.

An HSP is exquisitely aware of their own sensations, but may not be particularly able to understand the inner world of someone else. Whereas the HSP phenomenon is about direct perception, empaths have a more intuitive and internal experience that goes beyond stimulation. Consequently, an empath can be finely tuned to other people's emotions but have no issues with loud sounds, bright lights, or unpleasant textures like HSPs.

In short, empaths may share many traits with HSPs and introverts, but don't necessarily have to. Introverted empaths prefer having smaller groups of very good friends, quiet gatherings, and in-depth talk—and not too frequently. Extroverted empaths (less common, but they do exist) engage with others happily but may be more verbally expressive, taking less time to get overstimulated. HSPs can also look like empaths, but don't necessarily have to feel the emotions of others, a key trait of empaths.

A more concerning association, however, is that of empaths and what are called *codependents*. Critics of much of the new empath literature point to a stark similarity between being an empath and presenting symptoms of a damaging mental disorder. Here again we see a tussle for how empaths are to be defined and regarded—as victims or saviors? As superheroes or damaged people? As deluded or as possessing superior skills of perception?

A codependent is a person who gets involved in an unhealthy dynamic with another person (and sometimes a mental health disorder is involved, such as addiction). In this story, a codependent attaches themselves strongly to someone they feel compelled to "save," but ends up enabling them or getting sucked into their dysfunction.

Codependent people can carry enormous amounts of shame and guilt that lock them into patterns of behavior with others who have corresponding issues. For example, a husband might be abusive to his partner, but she may stay out of some misplaced sense of "helping" him—while not realizing her unconscious desire to hold on to a situation in which she is forever the good, selfless victim who can blame her persecutor for every failure in her life.

Codependency is a complicated and sensitive topic, but it can be extremely beneficial for empaths to understand these dynamics so that they can be honest with themselves. It is common today to see people talk about the relationship between empaths and narcissists as though narcissists are thoroughly evil people dead set on exploiting saintly empathic figures who are only trying to help. The trouble with this story is that it doesn't acknowledge the role that empaths unconsciously play to keep these toxic dynamics going. In pointing the finger at "narcs," they inadvertently disempower themselves, avoid solving the problem realistically, and avoid taking ownership for their own behavior.

What's the difference between an empath and a codependent?

Well, perhaps when empaths choose to remain in unhealthy situations and use empathy when boundaries would be more appropriate—they more closely resemble codependents. An empath can fall into a codependent dynamic, but this doesn't mean that this is what they *are*. It simply means that if they bring their abilities to an unhealthy relationship, those abilities will be warped and misused. After all, it is not really empathy to deliberately keep yourself in harmful situations, or to valiantly try to prevent other people from experiencing their own emotions or the consequences of their own actions. In fact, an empath who is functioning in this way could be said to be wasting their gifts.

It is tempting for many to simply say, "I'm suffering because I'm an empath," especially if this allows us to avoid other painful nuances and truths. An unhealthy empath may have desperately low self-esteem, low self-love, boundary issues, and even a "martyr complex," but this is because their innate empathy has not found a healthy outlet.

A well-adjusted, self-respecting empath can avoid toxic relationships without demonizing anyone, and without constructing narratives in which they are the blameless victims. In fact, many empaths find healing when they abandon the victim-aggressor-savior narrative and take ownership of the fact that they may be more prone than others to choose narcissistic partners (often wrongly phrased as "narcissists *prey* on empaths").

Codependency is not the same as being an empath, but a wounded empath can certainly behave in codependent ways. When an empath realizes that they cannot help everyone, and that they are not responsible for the emotions of others, they can recover and start to pick better partners. Rather than getting unconscious validation from being everyone's problem-solver, emotion sponge, or therapist, empaths can use their skills more maturely and start to embody the superhero rather than the supervictim!

Too Little Versus Too Much

On this note, let's dig a little deeper into some of these ideas that may be uncomfortable for people just starting to explore the idea of being an empath.

Because empaths have often found themselves in dramatic tangles with narcissists, suggestions have been made that they have more in common than they at first think. Whereas the narcissist has too little, the empath has too much—are they really two sides of the same coin? Or even more alarmingly, is being an empath really a form of *covert* narcissism (i.e. a hidden, less obvious form)?

A narcissist will see themselves as better than everyone else, and may conduct themselves with an air of entitlement and grandiosity, being self-interested, confident, and relatively unconcerned with others. Overt narcissists are the classic type—domineering, obsessed with their image, and baldly claiming their superiority, all the while having little respect or regard for others. A covert narcissist, however, might conceal these beliefs a lot better, and may even present as someone with low self-esteem.

They may be hypersensitive to criticism and positively unable to tolerate any rejection, only seeking the limelight out passively or indirectly. Rather than brashly pursuing fame and glory, they may simply work hard to avoid failure and rejection. Returning to the concept of projection, and the fact that empaths may frequently find themselves tangled up with those they feel are narcissistic, could it be that some empaths are really covert narcissists?

Few empaths would admit to it, even if it was true! But someone with a quiet superiority or smugness, a degree of self-absorption, sensitivity (to rejection), and passive aggression may use the label of empath to hide behind. They are not truly empathic (in fact, they may have low empathy and be terrible listeners) but they may falsely identify with the image of a Very Special empathic person because it aligns with their vision of being superior.

But, happily, the fact is that although narcissists can pretend to be empaths, they are not the same thing. It is simply a case, again, of having two distinct phenomena share some outward appearances. The main difference is, of course, in empathy. While the narcissist's eternal focus is (always!) themselves, an empath is genuinely capable of entering into another person's world with compassion and gentleness.

If you hear an "empath" emphasize how special, wonderful, unique, and different they are (i.e. how superior), you might wonder if they were a little narcissistic. Or it may be that the empath, having lived with abilities that were reviled and misunderstood for so long, is now feeling more empowered to be proud of who they are—it can get complicated.

Ultimately, an empath is a human being. They can have moments of selfishness, meanness, or of thinking quite highly of themselves. But in many ways, the empath is the *opposite* of the narcissist. While the world of the psychopath, sociopath, or narcissist has held some fascination for researchers and the general public alike, it would seem that it's more recently the other end of the spectrum that is receiving attention.

Could it be that people on the extreme ends of this continuum have merely been misunderstood by more "normal" people? Perhaps extreme empathy is so rare and outside the typical experience that people can't help but interpret it incorrectly—or doubt its existence entirely.

This is where the "super empath" enters the picture. Not only do some people resonate with the empath description, but others take it a step further and claim to be "super empaths"—people who are so deeply tuned into the experiences of others that they may completely blur the boundary between self and other.

Research done by psychologist Doctor Michael Banissy has focused on mirror-touch synesthesia (MTS)—finding that up to two percent of the population can literally feel another person's experience in their own bodies. When people with MTS see someone else being touched, they literally experience the sensation on their own skin. Studies done to investigate this phenomenon show that a handful of people are literally unable to differentiate between sensations experienced by themselves and by others, i.e. they get confused about who exactly is having an experience. This includes physical touch but possibly other aspects of empathy, too, such as cognitive, emotional, or even spiritual aspects.

The interesting thing, however, is that people with this ability *typically don't know they have it*—how could they if they believe that what they experience truly "belongs" to them? This has the curious effect of both confirming the existence of empaths but also calling into question the self-assessment of those who *claim* they have this ability.

It's also a less flattering portrait of an empath as a person who is *lacking* the ability to switch awareness between self and other, rather than possessing any extra ability. Someone with "overactive" empathy who has difficulty separating themselves from others can understandably become overwhelmed and stressed. Researchers have also noted that people with MTS may experience another person's emotions but may not be any better at understanding people because of this ability.

Again, it would seem that there are two main interpretations of the empath's experience—either that their abilities are a troubling oversensitivity that feels more like a disability, or that their empathic nature is a gift or superpower that allows them to reach wonderful heights of human potential. So, which is it? That depends on the empath.

Increasingly, self-identified empaths have been attempting to make real use of their gifts in the world, working with others as healers, counselors, and even spiritual teachers. They *consciously* use their ability to melt into another's emotional field for their benefit. Some now make their living from sharing their skills and abilities with others, converting what used to be a source of overwhelm and confusion into something that helps other people.

"Professional" empaths have discovered that their curse can become a gift, or even their life's work and calling. Having learned to work *with* rather than *against* their talents, some super empaths claim to be able to predict the future with some accuracy, receive communications from other souls or energies, heal and release emotional trauma—all very valuable in a world that has been described as "empathy-deficient"!

Some empaths have counterintuitively found a way to strengthen their boundaries and boost self-esteem by charging for their services as life coaches, therapists, or healers. The idea is that an overwhelmed, stressed empath is no good to anyone anyway—only one who understands and uses their gifts wisely has anything to offer humanity.

By using their unique sensitivity to improve other people's "emotional literacy," empaths take what could be a disability and work it into something truly enriching. So, is being an empath a curse or a fit? The answer may be obvious by now: it's *both*, depending on how well these abilities are nurtured. This leads us to the topic of our next chapter.

Takeaways

- What is the difference between empaths and what could be called an intense sense of empathy? In truth, they are highly related. They both involve the ability to place themselves in other people's shoes and experience the emotions along with them. They feel deeply and are sometimes unable to avoid being affected. It is not something that they must consciously summon; they are immersed in it, and it is the primary way in which they relate to the world and people. There can be said to be a few different types of empathy: cognitive, emotional, somatic, compassion, and spiritual.

- As we understand more about the human mind and how not everyone fits into a box, we have expanded definitions for what normal can be. It's important to distinguish between other new, expanded definitions to better understand what drives the empath. To be clear, there can be significant overlaps between these personality classifications, but there are also significant overlaps between the summer months and ice cream consumption. It doesn't always mean much. Highly Sensitive People are empaths without the focus on emotional energy, introverts prefer to spend more time alone, and codependents are empaths but with a savior complex and a lack of personal boundaries.
- Then we come to the narcissists, who can be said to be the polar opposite of empaths. Whereas the narcissist has too little, the empath has too much. Unfortunately, there is a special kind of chemistry between these two personality classifications that make them fit together in a fatal way.

Chapter Three. Self-Awareness, Self-Protection, and Self-Care

Empaths may find that their life paths are a little different from others', and that in order to use their attributes as the gifts they could potentially be, they first need to heal themselves and learn to understand how and why their hearts and minds work as they do. A young empath may struggle immensely as they "come out" into the world—they may have little understanding of why they're different, and the possibilities ahead of them.

What's needed is a framework to organize and understand the unique life path of the empath. When such a person is empowered, conscious, and deliberate, they can gain immense healing and integration within themselves, which then allows them to really switch on their "superpower"!

No two empath journeys will be the same, but advice from other empaths who have gone through their own awakenings can be enormously helpful. In a world that feels as though it's on a different channel entirely, it can become the empath's responsibility to work out their own worldview, and their own unique set of codes and ethics that help them navigate their own power.

Healthy empaths need to prioritize their own personal wellbeing and development, and they need to frame and nurture their gifts in a way that is meaningful and empowering for *them*. From those empaths who have walked the sometimes lonely and difficult path of coming to terms with who they are, we can take surprisingly consistent advice.

A common idea is to use your gifts with discernment, and to realize that you can empathize at will, *or choose not to.* You can learn to respect the emotional privacy of other people—just because you can see something, it doesn't mean they want to see it or be told about it or have it reflected back at them. And it also doesn't mean you have to pick their emotions up and take responsibility for them!

Empaths learn true self-worth and agency by knowing when and how to draw the lines between self and other. It's a strong and healthy empath who can say, "This is *yours*, not mine," and draw a line if necessary. Similarly, empaths themselves can be incredibly intense and even intrusive, encouraging a depth that other people may not be ready for or receptive to. Empaths have to respect this—boundaries go both ways. It's a good idea to never step into another person's emotional world unless invited. You *can*, but that doesn't mean you *should*.

Themes of responsibility, boundaries, and conscious ownership will crop up again and again for an empath. Knowing that a potential weakness is how your sense of self can easily blur, it is up to you to take responsibility for your own feelings while allowing others to take responsibility for theirs. In a great sea of emotion, it's your job to have the presence of mind to pause and ask what your "business" is, and what isn't. An overwhelmed empath can quickly lash out and blame others—but in fact, it is our responsibility to monitor our boundaries and to decide what we allow in and what we screen out for our own wellbeing.

Crucially, understand that feeling hurt doesn't necessarily mean that someone has hurt you. You have a choice in what boundaries and limits you set up for yourself. The greatest skill an empath can learn is to confidently set up boundaries without blame or judgment, and assert those boundaries when it matters.

An empath will naturally pick up on other's emotions. But it can take some experience, practice, and wisdom to *understand* what you're feeling and consciously channel that energy and experience. Where does this emotion come from? Is it yours or someone else's? Listen closely to emotions that arise as though they were messengers—respect and honor them as guests but allow them to flow freely once their message has been communicated.

Meditation can help empaths loosen their attachment to overwhelming emotions. It can be an enormous relief to really understand that emotions will pass, good or bad, and that you can always find a place of peace behind whatever mental and emotional fluctuations happen throughout the day.

Fellow empaths will tell you that your abilities are a gift, if you respect them. Push against or deny what you feel, and your feelings will become a source of suffering. Instead, trust and honor yourself. When you have a gut feeling, listen to it. So many of us feel that others don't listen to us or take us seriously, when all the while, we don't listen to ourselves or take our own intuition seriously! Pause regularly to "tune in." What are your feelings telling you about the situation, person, or information in front of you? Listen closely and have faith in what that voice tells you.

Finally, you may have noticed that to do all this takes time and effort. That's why you need alone time to practice proper empath self-care. An empath has a remarkable ability to self-heal, to almost counsel themselves—if they are given the time and space to do so. As an empath, it's your responsibility to *make* time for this vital aspect of your self-care.

There is never any need to be a martyr. Instead, allow yourself time to regularly step back, retreat, and process what you need to. Take the day off to do nothing. Contemplate. Read or journal quietly, or spend time in nature. Think of it as a metabolic function, like digestion—only on an emotional and spiritual level. You need to practice regular emotional hygiene to integrate feelings, release old emotions, and renew your sense of balance and harmony. *Then* you can go out in the world and help those you want to help!

Think of it as building up your energetic reserves. Whether it's nature, your connection to the divine, or simply rest and relaxation, honor the source of your renewal and "top up" frequently so you never run on empty. Your gut feeling is important here—listen to that voice telling you it's time to rest.

As you become more comfortable and confident being the unique person you are, you can start to think of emotions as flows of energy—not flows that dominate and overwhelm you, but flows that can be managed, directed, used for the purposes *you* decide to use them. This is where an empath taps into their real power. A healthy empath differs from an unhealthy one in one regard—they have taken conscious, loving ownership and responsibility for who they are and how their hearts and minds work.

You might find it helpful to literally draw up a list of things that feed your soul, and take the responsibility to make sure you're regularly getting enough of these "heart vitamins" to be the best empath you can be. Notice what leaves you feeling calm and balanced, and do more of that! It may be that you need to regularly go out into nature. Have a pet, buy a bouquet of flowers, do some gardening, or take a daily walk in the early morning, where you can drink up the beautiful peace and stillness of the natural world.

You may find that you're not so much of an introvert if you can regularly spend time with likeminded people with which you can form a conscious community or "tribe." Find friends who will understand your need for occasional alone time, or join online forums and groups of other empaths with whom you can share this aspect of your life with. Don't feel you have to "dumb down" on the topics that interest you—if you need intellectual, emotional, and spiritual stimulation, it's worth seeking those things out, whether from others, books, or online. It goes without saying that you should enter these spaces with healthy, intact boundaries—give yourself full permission to say no or walk away from people you know are not healthy for you.

If you have a romantic partner, you may need to do some work on not losing yourself in the intimacy. Communicate often to make your needs crystal clear. It's an act of self-care to compassionately communicate your need to retreat at times—never feel guilty for asking for it! A good partner will soon realize that an empath who can recharge at their own pace on their own terms is a happier, healthier partner with an almost endless capacity for love and connection.

As you develop, you may naturally gravitate toward mindfulness practices. These can put a shape and structure to daily self-care practices, acting like an anchor in a shifting world. A meditation practice can get you out of your head and into your body to release tension there and bring you back to the present. Regularly taking the time to self-soothe and calm yourself this way means you're strengthened and resilient in the face of sometimes strong emotions out there in the world. Daily habits like journaling, enjoyable hobbies, reading, quiet time, meditation or yoga, and nature walks are as important for emotional wellbeing as proper nutrition and exercise is for physical wellbeing.

Empathic Self-Protection

It's all about boundaries. It may feel sometimes like you can open up wide and accept the entire universe of feeling out there—but you are a human being, and you have *limits*. It's important that an empath has a self-care routine that keeps them topped up and healthy. But it's also important that they actively avoid things that can harm them, including their own and others' behaviors. Sometimes this necessarily involves actions that feel detrimental in the moment, but we are playing the long game.

There's a nasty habit that empaths can fall into: the tendency to sacrifice their own needs for someone else. This habit alone can undermine so much of the empath's power and wellbeing, and needs to be guarded against. At the root of this compulsion can be a deep-seated belief the empath has: *that they are responsible for making sure others don't feel pain.* Empaths can very easily feel downright responsible for the feelings and wellbeing of the people around them.

On the surface, it seems altruistic, but this is an incredibly damaging belief when you think about the implications and expectations it creates in someone. It can trap us, putting enormous pressure on us to manage the emotions of other people— despite the effect it has on *us*. The empath sacrifices easily—they may unconsciously take on the role of caretaker, savior, nurse, therapist, even parent.

If this is your tendency, you need to take care to see the situation with more objectivity: each of us can only be responsible for our own emotions. Suffering is unavoidable in this life . . . and who's to say what other people "should" experience? It's never really possible to do the work for someone else anyway—in fact, we can hold loved ones back when we shield them from the consequences of their own actions, or prevent them from feeling what they feel. Wanting to always be a good helper can drain us and paradoxically make us resent people, feeling obliged and trapped by their neediness (this is the codependent pattern we've already encountered).

You're an empath, but you can't read minds, and you can't predict the future (even if it sometimes seems that way!). Even if you love someone, you cannot protect them from all suffering all the time. We can barely protect ourselves from the same. Ask what stories you're telling yourself about your role in your relationship, family, or workplace. Is it a healthy, empowered story that respects the agency of others? It's not your job to save the world!

And even if it were, you'd only be able to do it if you saved yourself first. In our passion to fix others, are we neglecting ourselves? Another way to think about it is that you must yourself be happy and the most functional in order to help others more. We can't set ourselves on fire just to keep others warm.

Is it okay to be putting our own needs aside because it's okay if *we* suffer, as long as others don't? It may be far more empowering to trust other people to travel the paths they must, learn as and when they do, without our intervention. Nobody needs to be a hero. In fact, you can sometimes do the most by simply accepting and witnessing people as they are—without wanting to step in and make them how you think they *should* be.

When reading the above, you may notice that the "protection" is coming, essentially, from inside you, the empath. This is important. When some empaths talk about "protecting" themselves from others, they unconsciously paint others as harmful, toxic, insensitive, less evolved, or somehow unkind.

This is a trap not only because it's seldom true (people are allowed to feel as they feel, and simply because they happen to infringe on you or disagree with you doesn't make them lesser or toxic) but also because it disempowers the empath and makes them feel that they are weak and small, lost in a hostile world that can actively hurt them unless they shut down or close off. This is a type of learned behavior that leads to the empath feeling helpless and like a victim. Nothing could be further from the truth.

Protection for an empath is more accurately the adoption of a healthy, boundaried mindset, rather than seeing other people or their emotions as enemies (which is profoundly unempathetic, when you think about it). It has nothing to do with other people, in other words, and everything to do with *you* and the limits you place for yourself. Rather than framing your abilities as a weakness or something that allows you to be threatened and overwhelmed, understand your orientation as a fact of life that can be managed and used wisely—if only you take active and conscious responsibility for it.

This means releasing blame, judgment, or fear of others—these are not things we can control, and neither are they what we should expect to change or fix. When we have firm boundaries that we can trust and honor, it doesn't matter what *other people's* behavior is. It doesn't matter if they are narcissists, psychopaths, energy vampires, or just plain mean. Because we are in control.

So, in this spirit, preventing overload is simply taking ownership of your own unique way of absorbing and processing information and placing appropriate limits for your own wellbeing. You need never feel like a victim! If you are feeling rushed, fatigued, stressed out, and aggravated with noise, crowds, arguing, lack of sleep, bad food, and so on, it is not these things in themselves that are the problem, but our choice to put ourselves in those situations.

If you know that low blood sugar, a bad night's sleep, and a morning spent in traffic will likely put you in a bad frame of mind, it is your responsibility to make sure you step away and rest. It is *not* the fault of the next person who overwhelms you, and the solution is never to shut them out as though they were the problem.

Turn your exquisitely fine-tuned sensitivities inward and monitor your inner state. Are you getting exhausted? Time to pause and recalibrate. Protection only becomes necessary long after a boundary is violated (or not there in the first place!) or you're already emptied out and unhappy. The only one who can take charge of the abilities you have is you.

So, show yourself some love by taking the time to learn what makes you feel better, and what doesn't. Learn what your warning signs, red flags, and triggers are. Empaths are entirely in tune with their inner state of being and emotions, so this step should not be difficult. You likely already have a good sense of who or what situations make you feel stressed, anxious, unhappy, or otherwise in a mood you'd rather not be in. There is no need to deeply introspect here; you merely need to take a quick inventory of who tends to drain or energize you.

An empath who feels as though they need to constantly bunker down in a quiet room somewhere far away from people (i.e. protect or shield themselves) has likely disregarded their *own* boundaries long before anyone else did. Again, the courage, self-awareness, and self-respect needed to set up good boundaries is what makes the difference.

You could choose to do a meditation or visualization where you imagine yourself being recharged and refreshed by rays of energy coming from the earth, the sun, or your own heart. Imagine you have a "spiritual immune system" that works best when you are healthy. Rather than dwell on the "energy vampires" who are seeking to attack and undermine you, draw your attention instead to a more appropriate realm of your control: yourself.

Become curious about the ways that you attract, encourage, allow, or agree to feeling drained or taken advantage of. What kind of unconscious contracts have you set up with others, or in what ways have you unconsciously brought about your current lack of energy? If all else fails, analyze your schedule or write down a list of your recent activities, and a pattern will likely soon emerge.

If you're feeling flooded or overwhelmed, or as though a boundary has been breached, your job is not to blame someone else but look to your own sense of self and boundaries. Have you properly drawn and communicated those boundaries? Yes, it's difficult, but the question still remains—did you properly communicate boundaries in the exact manner that you intended to, and was it received in that way?

Or do you, in some unconscious way, derive a sense of validation from defining yourself as fundamentally good and victimized, while those you dislike are framed as vampiric, narcissistic, even evil? These are some of the dynamics that a less than ideal childhood, or codependency, can easily give rise to. These are not easy things to think about, but they present a greater chance for true empowerment for an empath, well beyond merely feeling like you can hide away or shield from those parts of the world you dislike. Remember—with mature, healthy boundaries, there is never a *need* to shield or protect.

A well-developed empath will know that their state of mind and their energy levels are of prime importance. Eating well, resting, finding enough joy and gratitude in life, and so on—these are all things that build resilience and liberation. Think about the most optimal way to organize a calendar with no commitments yet for the coming week. You'd schedule your own priorities and needs in pen, while everything else would fit around them. This type of self-prioritization is a kind of boundary-setting.

Commit to finding your "medicine" and give yourself as much as you need—in fact, it might be more helpful to view these things as your air, food, and water. Necessities. Unplug and go outside with bare feet on the earth, gaze at the stars, swim in the ocean, or spend some time listening to the whispering of trees. "Grounding" is not just something you can do in nature—any time you are feeling your energy levels deplete or your mood worsen, simply pause, connect to deep breaths, and relax.

Meditate, even if only for a few moments. Be an empty sky and see the emotions passing over it like clouds. Observe your feelings crashing over you like a wave, and then dissipate back into nothing. All stress, worry, angst . . . it's all simply passing weather. Connect to the feeling of *being* the clear, boundless, serene blue sky under it all.

Tranquility doesn't mean nothing ever happens or that you no longer tolerate negative emotions. It simply means you don't cling to them as tightly, or become overly attached or identified with them. You can let them pass, flow through. You are anchored within yourself and your own deep, unshakeable sense of wellbeing. In this state, you will not be subject to the manipulations of narcissists, the drama of other people's emotions, the noise of the chaotic world.

As an empath, you are open and witness to a world of emotion and feeling, and you can only face the emotions of others with the same attitude as you have to your own emotions. If you are fearful, suspicious, uncomfortable, or doubtful about who you are, how else could you be when you encounter other peoples' emotions? Other people can sometimes reflect our own beliefs and feelings back to us. That's why many empaths find that when they prioritize their own emotional wellbeing, it's far, far easier to navigate the bluster and chaos of other people's emotions.

Understand the importance of setting realistic boundaries, and make sure to give yourself plenty of time apart so you can find your own inner balance and equanimity.

Don't force yourself to have relationships with people who don't understand you, or worse, don't care about you. Don't agree to any kind of relationship where you have to sacrifice or bend over backward. Choose people who will value you, not those who you constantly feel you have to change for.

Say no when you need to, and don't feel guilty about who might not like hearing it. This applies to relationships too—you're *always* allowed to end a relationship that isn't working for you. Yes, feelings of guilt, obligation, and duty will attempt to anchor you to some people. This is another subtle way that we are putting the mere *desires* of someone else above our own *needs*. These should not be equally weighed.

Watch your energy levels very, very closely. Take note every time you feel an abrupt change or mood shift, and ask why. What you want is to make life flow as smoothly and with as much balance as possible. Avoid extremes, bad habits, alcohol or overeating, dramatic friends, social media binges, horror movies, and so on.

Make it a daily commitment to do something kind for yourself. Tune in and show yourself some love. Do you need a nap, a treat, or to talk with a loved one?

Energy Management

As an empath, your world can be understood as a flowing and shifting ocean of energy. Empaths are already *aware* of emotions all around them, but it can sometimes take extra effort to skillfully manage these experiences—a little like learning to navigate a boat on that rocky ocean!

A practical tip is to physically move yourself away from anything that threatens to overwhelm you. Don't worry about asking permission. Just step away if you need to. Move away from a noisy, aggressive TV show, a rowdy group of people, or a person who has decided to "dump" their negative emotions on you. If you're still learning to master boundaries, it can be easy at first to literally and physically put distance between yourself and something you feel unable to cope with.

Take deep breaths, or practice a quick bit of grounding meditation. Get back in your body and notice how you feel. Center yourself and decide how you *want* to feel. Visualize your own strong, healthy boundaries as a fearsome jaguar protecting you, or an unbreakable barrier that cannot be interfered with by other people. You may find that you are actually better able to deal with difficult things in your field of awareness if you can first take a few moments to calm and recalibrate yourself.

Another practical skill is to get good at saying no. It's a complete sentence! This means you never have to justify, explain, beg, plead, or apologize when affirming a boundary. If you're at work, for example, and asked to take on unpaid overtime, there's nothing wrong with calmly saying, "Hm, I'm sorry, but that won't be possible. I'll be able to take a look tomorrow morning when I get in, though." In a relationship, it's okay to say, "I love you, but I'm going to need some alone time this evening."

If you're cornered by a person who wants to use you as a therapist, don't be afraid to interrupt a long rant and tell them you'll talk to them some other time. Most importantly, don't suffer in silence and keep quiet when your intuition is telling you to get away from a situation. These situations are draining for normal folk—multiply the negative feelings threefold for yourself, and you can start to see just how much you need to manage your emotional energy.

In time, you'll get better at monitoring the flow of energy into and out of your body. It's so much more than putting up a shield to block out unwanted sensations. It's asking yourself what you actively *need* and taking steps to ensure you get it. Plan ahead if you expect a difficult encounter, be empowered enough to state your needs and boundaries clearly to others, and take action to give yourself rest and retreat when you need it. Don't get into the habit of making commitments you don't want to keep.

Prevent overload by regularly pausing to check in with yourself—and honoring what you need in every moment. You might be surprised to see that people respond well— the next time you want to leave a party or social gathering, explain (honestly!) that you're feeling a little depleted energy-wise, rather than making up an obvious excuse. You'll feel a lot better for being sincere and may discover that often the only person keeping you in an uncomfortable situation is yourself!

A healthy empath is the one who has taken the time to set up a lifestyle for themselves that supports rather than drains them. Unless you deliberately make room for quiet time and meditation, nobody else will do it for you, and it will fall to the bottom of the list of priorities. Don't wait until you are burnt out and completely exhausted to give yourself some TLC. Take breaks as often as you need to, and not on some schedule someone else sets for you.

Take your own car to events so that you can leave when you want to. Don't say yes to things out of guilt and then resent having to follow through. Sleep enough, avoid binging, drinking alcohol, or wasting hours online (which could be as depleting as time spent in a massive crowd). Pace yourself, stay hydrated, and remember to breathe!

If you make your own home a personal sanctuary, you can use it as an emotional and spiritual "checkpoint"—burn incense or light a candle, play gentle music, surround yourself with textures and colors you love, and bring in some nature in the form of plants and flowers to ground and calm you.

You might even like to dedicate spaces in your home that are just for rest and relaxation—a shielded reading corner with comfy cushions and a blanket, a spare room where you can do yoga and stretch, or a spot outside where you can just go to breathe, put your bare feet in the grass, and listen to the birds. Some empaths routinely go on mini-retreats, go offline or technology-free for a few days, or take long, long walks or trips alone to recalibrate their energy levels.

The idea is to remove all outside noise, all external stimulation, so that you can simply feel what *you* feel. When you're calm and alone, you can start to ask, "Is this sensation mine or someone else's? Do I want to feel it or can I let it go?" You can often tell that an emotion is absorbed from outside of yourself if it comes on quickly but disappears the moment you remove yourself from the stimulus.

Consciously decide to let go of emotions you don't want or need—in your body as well as your mind. Learn to scan your body and conduct min-audits throughout the day to see where your energy level is and how you're feeling. Notice, also, if you're telling yourself any stories about how you should feel, or are getting caught up in fear, guilt, or shame. Realize that all these things are a choice, and give yourself the space to choose how you'd really like to feel.

Warding off Fatigue

You may recall that empathy can be cognitive, emotional, spiritual, or somatic (physical), and so it follows that empaths may show the same variation. Most empaths predominantly experience other people's emotions, but there are some out there who also or even primarily experience other people's physical realities as their own. Physical empaths may even manifest illnesses and symptoms of the people around them, coming to label themselves with diseases that more rightly belong to the people they've absorbed them from.

Have you ever felt physically exhausted after spending time with someone, but couldn't quite say why? Do crowds often make you feel sick, hungover, exhausted, or even in pain? Perhaps you feel chronically tired but sleep well, eat well, and have nothing to explain why you should feel so run down all the time.

Unexplained symptoms like this can often point to your empathic abilities taking a physical form. Simply being in the proximity of someone else can leave somatic empaths feeling drained and ill. Relax—this doesn't mean you're a hypochondriac, weakling, or malingerer. It's not "all in your head," either. Rather, you are hosting pain that more rightly belongs to other people—and, importantly, you don't have to put up with it.

Sometimes, all you need to do is be conscious enough to ask symptoms that cross your conscious awareness, "Where do you come from? What are you about?" and notice the answer. Remove yourself from people or situations you suspect are causing you strain and see what happens. Some people have body parts or systems that are more susceptible to absorbing unwell energy from others.

If you know you typically get headaches or that you always seem to feel the trouble in your stomach, take action to pay extra attention to these areas and give yourself the support you need. Remember to keep breathing—breathing allows fresh oxygen into every part of your body, slows your thoughts, and gives you a moment to become aware of and release any unwanted tension.

The mind is an incredibly powerful thing. It's easy to imagine that emotions are simply some abstract, free-floating entities, but more often than not, they are *embodied*.

Whether yours or someone else's, take the time to regularly release tension and negative emotions from your body. During meditation, ask where your body is tense and unhappy, and zoom in your awareness onto these areas.

Visualize sending love and healing to where it's needed, breathe deeply, and let the pain go. You may need to strengthen or redraw your boundaries to make sure that you're not taking on other people's stress, suffering, or pain. If you routinely take on the illness and emotions of others, you may find yourself with a general background sense of being exhausted and run down, i.e. chronic fatigue.

It may be that you have absorbed a specific symptom from someone else, or that you are generally overwhelmed by an onslaught of emotional energy from many different people, and feel exhausted as a result. This is "compassion fatigue," but is more accurately understood as a sign that your boundaries and self-care need some work. Remember that compassion is not an infinite resource and that you, as a human being, have physical needs and limits that will result in illness if not respected.

Working with other people's strong emotions, illness, pain, or trauma can cause burn out, and can build up over time until you feel like you can't even say what's wrong anymore, you just feel completely empty and numb. An overburdened heart can quickly become apathetic, irritable, or angry.

Though empathizing with others comes naturally, it is *not possible or desirable* to be a caregiver, savior, rescuer, or nurturer full time, with no rest or recuperation of our own. Unbalanced empaths can be drawn to those who are suffering, and get embroiled in depleting themselves trying to help them. They can sacrifice themselves, forging their own needs until there isn't much left to give anyway—this is an empath who has not learned to manage and take responsibility for the flow of energy around them. Replacing the natural empathy will be exhaustion, resentment, anxiety, avoidance, and more. In other words, an empath *can* care too much, and it's not pretty when it happens.

The way to manage illness and fatigue is to not let it happen in the first place. This can be done with a strong sense of self-awareness that can allow you to make minor "course corrections" as you navigate the world. Know thyself. Know your limits and your needs. Know the signs that you're approaching your limits, and know what you need to do to recuperate and refresh. Your only real responsibility is to maintain good self-care—put yourself first, knowing that a broken, burned-out healer is no healer at all!

Constantly check in with your body, heart, and mind and see what is needed. Practice giving to yourself first before you deign to help others. In time, you might see that you can do more for others by being well yourself, by letting people feel what they feel, and by not interfering and preventing others from suffering as though it's your soul's duty. It isn't!

Resist the temptation to valorize exhaustion that comes from caring too much. It's not a badge of honor to neglect the self in service of someone else's (perceived) need. What's more, you seldom help someone by confirming their victim status and reinforcing your role in their life as savior. Have enough respect for others to let them walk the path they are walking, while turning your attention to the challenges on your own path.

On a related note, empaths can find enormous growth and healing in putting down the cater role for a moment and deliberately asking for help from others instead. Acknowledge when you feel overwhelmed, scared, alone. Ask for guidance and enjoy being taken care of by someone else for a change! You will know you are a healthy, balanced empath when giving and caring is a source of joy for you, and not something that feels like it diminishes or empties you. Compassion is a wonderful thing, but it needs to be done with care, wisdom, and skill. Balance it always with *compassion for yourself,* and you will never again experience your empathic abilities as a source of fatigue.

The Lurking Past

Finally, even if there was no direct or obvious trauma, the prevailing trait of the empath is to be affected more than the typical degree. Thus, empaths are more likely to experience PTSD and the effects of trauma, not least of all because their bodies may be more often in a cortisol-heavy "fight or flight" mode or inundated with information coming their way. It doesn't require being in a warzone or an extensive history of early childhood trauma, though these things may have helped spur and develop their empathic abilities.

Trauma can be said to be the innermost layer that empaths must pay special attention to. If trauma is a big part of your experience as an empath, you may need to go a little further in your self-care.

Trauma can cover a range of upsetting experiences, from being bullied and told to "stop being so sensitive" right through to physical, emotional, or sexual abuse. A sensitive or empathic child can even experience relatively normal households as upsetting if they are loud, unsupportive, or chaotic, leading them to internalize some degree of trauma around their sensitivities. Don't forget that we are looking at emotions and negativity as if wearing a hearing aid or looking through binoculars.

Things are magnified, and for our purposes, we should broaden the definition of trauma to those *past experiences that subconsciously make us react in strong ways against our intentions.* Most often these things put us into a state of heightened arousal that is not pleasant to constantly experience.

Having to constantly be on guard emotionally can be understood as *hypervigilance*, and is accompanied by a central nervous system that is always switched on and on the lookout for a new threat to protect against. These early experiences can leave adult empaths dealing with a range of anxiety disorders later in life. They may even find themselves flashing back to old traumas whenever they encounter overwhelming or threatening stimuli in the present day. Cue the imagery of the war veteran who goes into a state of panic whenever they hear a loud sound that in some way resembles a shooting gun sound.

In this state of mind, an empath can feel constantly on edge, unable to relax, and as though they are under threat from every direction. In a world of hyperstimulation, an empath can feel positively frazzled and triggered into reliving past trauma.

Thankfully, there are many ways for empaths to heal and integrate these early experiences. Awareness and understanding are of utmost importance. Empaths may know that they are feeling something, but without a clear attribution, this is information that you cannot do anything with. A common method to do this is to journal regularly to help unpack and sort through emotions. Any time there is a large emotion, or even a notable emotion, don't you dare tell yourself that it didn't matter or that it's not a big deal.

These reactions come from somewhere, and its often only through writing out our feelings and thoughts that we can understand what we truly think, and the connection between our pasts, our thoughts, our beliefs, and finally, our actions. Most of us are operating on a type of autopilot, where we know we have thoughts, and we can see the results of our actions, but we don't consider the connection between the two.

Suppose someone brushes up against your neck inadvertently, and you have a huge reaction that makes your heart race and your palms sweat. This is not something to be swept under the rug, and we should consider analyzing the aforementioned process: our pasts, thoughts, beliefs, and finally, actions. We are starting at the end of the process with only breadcrumbs (actions), but often, the answer lies beneath our very noses.

You can also think of yourself as a child and take on the position of an older, wiser adult who can now go back and re-parent yourself. What would you tell your inner child? What did they need back then and how can you give it to yourself now? This exercise makes you step outside your own experience and view things a bit more objectively and in a more solution-oriented manner. Instead of being caught in the minutiae of your own situation, take a step back and understand the whole picture.

As emotions surface, it's important to accept them and let them flow through— this is how you learn about yourself. Speak to a trusted friend or even a therapist, and don't judge or undermine your experience. In time, you may start to gain clarity on ways that you'd like to be different in your day-to-day life. Commit to taking small, healing actions for yourself. Set a boundary with that intrusive, entitled person at work. Speak up in your relationship about something you're unhappy about. Let go of things that are only in your life because you feel obliged and guilty.

Know that whenever you experience strong emotions, you can always pause, take a deep breath, and anchor back in the moment. You *always* have that power. Take it slow and go easy on yourself. Nobody ever healed without hearty doses of compassion, so give yourself time and patience to heal—you deserve it! As an empath, you are just as vulnerable to the whole gamut of mental health issues as everyone else, if not more so. For those who feel deeply, things like depression and anxiety can be wildly disorienting and quickly take over. This is why it's so important for empaths to take care of themselves all the time, every day, and not wait until they feel overwhelmed and unwell.

Because of their heightened sensitivity, empaths can be particularly vulnerable to anxiety and panic attacks, which can spiral rapidly and leave them feeling devastated and raw emotionally. Here, an empath needs to have the skills to arrest a panic spiral in its tracks, soothe themselves, and ground in the present moment. A good practice is to learn to do "sensory gating," which is the ability to filter out noise and all kinds of external stimulation that is excessive or irrelevant. This prevents overload and gives you an immense sense of relief and empowerment. The easiest way to do this is to cultivate and work with silence, but we can apply this sort of principle to our scheduling, calendaring, and work priority practices.

Know that you can remove yourself, literally, emotionally, or even spiritually, from the noise and bustle of life. Take a step back from overwhelming stimuli. Imagine your conscious awareness and attention is a beam of light that you can willingly focus on certain stimuli and not others. Turn the dial down on noises, ideas, emotions, or images that you don't care about. As you might have imagined, meditation of all kinds will help you develop this ability, as will simply sitting quietly and experimenting with where your awareness moves and flows with external stimuli.

You might also find it helps to get noise-cancelling earphones and listen to peaceful music or nature sounds to help you focus and tune out noise and distractions. Go into nature (barefoot if possible) and empty your mind, imagining it filling up again with clean, fresh silence, like spring water. Silence can be found in a tranquil Epsom salt bath, or by taking a few moments to burn some incense, eyes closed, focusing on nothing in the world but its aroma.

Silence is also close allies with darkness. Sit peacefully outside under a dark sky, or meditate in a dark room or with a blindfold so as to remove sight as a source of stimulation. This will allow you to more easily tune into your body, scents, inner sensations, and sounds. Yogic breathing and chanting can be a great way to empty the heart and mind and open up to healing. Focus only on the breath and the sound of your voice—so simple and yet so powerful in the moment.

Many empaths notice that when they turn off the outside world, their own inner worlds can wake up, and they feel more creative and expressive. Take a holiday from social media, the news, or the internet in general. Forego noisy music and TV and slow right down. You may be surprised to find that your body knows exactly how to heal and rebalance, if only given a moment of calm to do it.

Finally, empaths often find themselves using addiction to help with trauma.

Overstimulation can be so overwhelming that they tend to self-medicate to numb themselves, whether that's with food, substances, alcohol, sex, shopping, or any other addictive behavior. The idea is that all this *switches off* empathy and brings relief. But it's a false relief, and will eventually cause more harm than good. These coping mechanisms do more bad than good.

The first step to unraveling addiction and empathy is to be aware of how overstimulation is causing the desire to numb out with an addictive behavior or substance. It's a problem if you find yourself wanting to stop but unable to, or if the addiction is damaging relationships, work, or your health. You may need to work with a therapist to identify triggers and find genuine and healthy sources of self-care instead.

An empath can release addictive behaviors if they understand *why* they're there in the first place, and how they can get their needs met more directly instead. This takes honesty (no shame!) and the willingness to deal with whatever overload is causing you to depend on your addictions—most roads lead back to the need for self-awareness and addressing of internal traumas. Be crystal clear about the extent of your addiction and take ownership of it, but have self-compassion. Once you understand that your addiction can never give you the sense of wholeness and peace you crave, you can begin to let it go. For those empaths who are battling addiction, the necessity of self-care is even more important.

Takeaways

- Healthy empaths need to prioritize their own personal wellbeing and development, and they need to frame and nurture their gifts in a way that is meaningful and empowering for *them*. A common idea is to use your gifts with discernment, and to realize that you can empathize at will, *or choose not to.* Empaths learn true self-worth and agency by knowing when and how to draw the lines between self and other. This all points to one important concept in personal relationships: boundaries.

- Empaths can very easily feel downright responsible for the feelings and wellbeing of the people around them. But this is a boundary-less mindset, and it makes you a servant to the people around you, while ignoring your own needs. It is necessary to self-prioritize.
- Empaths also need to be cognizant of their energy and fatigue levels. Both of these can easily lead to a level of overwhelm that can be incapacitating. And for what, a lack of self-awareness? This is a tactic of self-protection, just like making sure that you have enough gas in your car's tank. Not only do empaths have to worry about normal fatigue, but also absorbing emotion and stress from others, and even compassion fatigue. This can all be accomplished with a growing comfort with saying no, strategic scheduling, and simply knowing your needs.
- Finally, empaths must be especially careful that their actions are not influenced by past traumas. Things are magnified, and for our purposes, we should broaden the definition of trauma

to those *past experiences that subconsciously make us react in strong ways against our intentions.* Most often these things put us into a state of heightened arousal that is not pleasant to constantly experience, and adds to overwhelm and anxiety.

Chapter Four. Empath Survival Tactics

This brings us neatly to what might be the most important work for an empath—figuring out how to cultivate a life that really works for them. We've considered both the blessings and curses that come with being an empath, and looked in detail at how an empath can protect themselves, maintain healthy boundaries, and learn to give themselves what they need for their wellbeing. At some point, an empath might want to turn their attention from finding ways to manage and mitigate their abilities, to thinking about ways to *optimize* them. In other words, the empath can't keep putting up defenses and blocks to the loud and noisy world. He or she must simply learn to operate better within it.

Being an empath can be hard if there is unresolved trauma or a lack of self-care and understanding. But once an empath learns to find their equilibrium and is routinely able to manage their own energy levels, unique sensitivities, and wants and needs, then empathy starts to look like a potential superpower—something that can add immense value and depth to life.

Empaths who are just learning about themselves may find it helpful at first to use certain labels and models to talk about their uncommon experiences. They may even find it beneficial to see and acknowledge the ways that they may have felt victimized, unsupported, misunderstood, sidelined, or demonized by the world at large. But eventually, an empath deeply connected to their own source and power will resist narratives in which they are weak victims.

They will soon start to appreciate their own gifts and see the power and potential in being able to feel deeply. They will start to make decisions for themselves, to put their wellbeing as a priority, and decide what their experiences mean in the bigger picture.

If an empath can take ownership of who they are and nurture their talents, those talents can be immensely beneficial for them and for everyone: optimism, compassion, intuition, cooperativeness, conscientiousness, good communication skills, spiritual intelligence, sensitivity, creativity—who wouldn't want to take full advantage of such a skill set? For the empath who is still healing, integrating and learning about themselves, the temptation may be to hide away, to downplay their needs and talents, to retreat. And this may be necessary as you learn to manage a bigger-than-normal capacity for emotional awareness.

But other empaths may find themselves facing another question with time: aren't they needed in the world in some way? What are they really here to do? Is there not a place for them in this world, and might it even be that their way of looking at the world is very much valued and needed right now?

Asking these questions can be the first step for an empath to realize how valuable they really are, and to start taking responsibility for how they can better serve themselves and the world in general. An empath may look at the world and see a cruel, irrational, heartless place, and decide to retreat and hide, but on the other hand, doesn't the cruel, irrational, and heartless world *need* more empaths?

As an empath, you can define yourself as you please. You can see the way you are as a disability, flaw, or weakness. You could use your skills as an excuse, as an exercise in ego, or a sophisticated way to project onto others and avoid your own emotional demons. Or, you could be grateful for your powers and see them as a precious gift, privilege, and even a responsibility.

What story do you want to tell? What do you want to teach and learn? In living your life, what do you want to show others or encourage or nurture? The first step is awareness—crystal clear and honest awareness of who you are, what you want, and where your weaknesses are. The next step is to trust yourself; trust your intuition, trust your body, and trust that voce inside that is guiding you. Be on guard for falling into the victim role or passively blaming others. Know that your self-esteem and worth come from a source much deeper than the label "empath" and everything it means.

As a matter of regular spiritual and emotional hygiene, maintain your boundaries like your life depends on it—because it does! Seek nature, meditate, breathe. Feed yourself—body and soul. Release ideas of yourself as an emotional punching bag or ultra-delicate flower.

See yourself instead as a transmuter of energy, an alchemist, a superb instrument that can use intention, love, and pure awareness to convert darkness into light. Be grateful for who you are and what you see and feel—you'd probably not want it any other way. At the end of the day, an empath's most powerful tool is love. Love for themselves and others. Deep, powerful love that cleanses, heals, and elevates everything it touches. This is a power worth protecting and maintaining!

When an empath struggles, wrestles with past trauma, or gets embroiled in dramas not their own because of weak boundaries or poor self-esteem, their talents are wasted. Their light is hidden. It is not merely the job of an empath to heal and find a way to "survive" in a hostile world. The true goal of an empath is to *thrive* as they are, to find a home for their abilities, to fulfill their potential and offer their gifts to a world that needs and wants them. With love and awareness, baby steps, and plenty of self-compassion, an empath can learn to live a profoundly deep, beautiful, and joyful life. Isn't it wonderful to be open, to feel and experience, to have a big heart to drink it all in?

On Defending Your Needs

As an empath taking charge of their gifts, you may need to tune into a deeper spiritual understanding of your place in the world, and a higher-level understanding of what role your empathy plays in the grand scheme of life—specifically with other people, something that cannot be avoided and instead should be optimized.

But all of this must develop in tandem with practical, real-world skills here and now, with people who may or may not understand or appreciate your abilities. We've already discussed the necessity of setting boundaries, but for those of us who have taken an unwitting "doormat" role in other peoples' eyes, *how* exactly do you do that?

In fact, taking a step back, what are some best practices for how empaths should be interacting with others, given the gifts and curses?

First, expect that maintaining boundaries is ongoing work. Little and often is better than allowing something to encroach bit by bit and then taking drastic action only when you feel really violated. Tell yourself as often as necessary, "I have a right to my own boundaries," and really feel into that sensation of perfect, non-negotiable self-respect.

Boundaries are not something that only mean or stingy people have, and most importantly, nobody can make them on your behalf. *You* are in control of your own energy, of what comes in and out. Is it uncomfortable? Certainly. But it helps to again take stock of what is at risk: your *needs*, or someone's mere *desires*. Take the time to contemplate, meditate, or journal on the following questions as often as necessary:

- What do *I* want here (regardless of what others want!)? And if this is something I do not want, what is actually making me feel compelled to do it?
- How do I want to feel right now?
- What is me and what is not me? (Or, what is "my business" and what has nothing to do with me?)
- What am I truly responsible for in this moment, and how can I affirm that?
- Where are my current boundaries, and what does it feel like to have them?

- Have I compromised myself, and why? How can I prevent it in the future?
- What is my body telling me about where I've drawn the boundary between self and other?
- Have I honored my own limitations?
- What do I really find acceptable, right, true, correct, or permissible, and have I communicated that effectively?
- Am I allowing my boundaries to be violated from a sense of guilt, shame, or fear?
- Am I allowing some of my needs to go unmet, and why?
- Can I forgive myself for learning, and be compassionate with the path I'm on?

By making the above considerations more and more automatic, you will learn to state your needs and limits calmly and without guilt. And other people will respond to it. You don't have to block anyone out or go into a safe bubble; you don't have to be mean or stop caring. You simply make sure that your needs are acknowledged, and that you never do anything that you don't want to do.

You can say, for example, "I'm sorry, but I don't think I want to do that," or, "I see what you're saying, but I don't really agree," or, "That's enough for me for now. I'm going to take a break." This is your bubble that you should draw a line around, because no one else is going to do it for you.

Crucially, it can be even harder to say no to people we really love and care about. We fear we may be acting without compassion, or that another person's suffering is somehow our fault if we don't step in to help. But a great moment of enlightenment comes for an empath when they realize they can still offer compassion without compromising themselves.

In fact, sometimes we can care and help *more* effectively when our boundaries are healthy and mature. We can recognize that sometimes the greatest gift we can give to someone else is to allow them to learn the life lessons they're meant to learn, without us rushing in to relieve them of suffering.

You know deep down inside that this just creates a cycle of dependence and in fact codependence, and the choice is always yours whether to engage or not— temporary unhappiness notwithstanding.

Saying no is a key skill for every empath. It's a sign that you value yourself and others, that you're in control. Saying no (and meaning it) means we honor our gifts by asking what we can realistically do for others, keeping our own wellbeing in the equation, too. An empowered no is a very pragmatic, honest thing. When it comes from a place of self-respect, most people will follow suit and respect that boundary.

But some won't. What do you do when people who are used to having you always say yes suddenly don't like you saying no? Someone who wants to manipulate you could resort to guilt-tripping, to asking over and over, to getting angry, to insulting you, or simply to ramping up their suffering in an attempt to push your pity buttons. And it may well work—empaths will go to great lengths to avoid conflict, to make sure someone doesn't feel bad. But you deserve better. Go quiet in yourself and listen. And at the end of the day, ask yourself those same questions from the beginning of the chapter, the primary one being "Is this what I actually want?"

Just understand that there is never going to be a graceful way to invoke your needs if it clashes with someone else's. It will necessarily feel bad, uncomfortable, guilty, and tense. But can you achieve an amazing body without some sort of sacrifice and pain? It is the same principle, and if you can shift your expectations, it should be a little bit easier.

If you don't feel empowered, respected, or heard, you may want to ask yourself if this is a situation or person you want to keep in your life. Do you want to be a caring, healing force in the life of someone who just sees you as free therapy, a dumping ground, or someone they can use to offload their miseries onto without caring how it affects them? Is that your role in people's lives?

Here is another evaluative question to understand your role—do you tend to know a lot about other people, while they tend to know relatively little about you? This isn't an unequal information exchange that occurs by accident. It occurs because you are the emotional sponge, they are the dumping truck, and it only goes in one direction.

Think about it this way: wouldn't you rather expend your empathy somewhere where it will be truly appreciated and needed? If we're honest with ourselves, we're not "helping" people by letting them take advantage of us, playing savior to them, or being an endless punching bag.

You can say no and then step away. You don't have to explain yourself, do something else to make the person feel better, act sheepish and sorry, or anything else. Simply state your boundary and notice the uncomfortable feelings, if any. Don't give into any feelings that tell you you're bad for drawing a line. Know that with repeated practice, it will get easier to stand calmly in your own self-respect.

Of course, real life can be a big, messy grey area sometimes and it can be genuinely difficult to know where your obligations end and where exactly to draw a line with someone who you sincerely care about. What's more, every human has to encounter conflict and disagreement at some point or other, so it's worth preparing beforehand as an empath and figuring out how to respond.

Conflict can be quick and intense, but it's manageable if you have a plan to deal with it. You may need to take a moment to remind yourself—sometimes even verbally, literally—that you are not responsible for the emotions of others. Where possible, take a breather and step away so you can re-center and have a moment of meditation.

Visualize yourself as made of Teflon and all the swirling emotions as failing to stick to you—you can examine the details later when you're calmer, but make a conscious effort not to attach to anything for the time being. Keep things simple and realign to your boundaries, and then allow lots and lots of space.

Simply notice what is happening (turn that superpower on!) and allow feelings to simply be what they are. Listen and accept without fear or judgment. One of the biggest things you can do to manage conflict is to stop telling yourself that conflict is unbearable, a problem, or something terrible that you want to run away from. Know that with your boundaries and an open heart, you can manage any conflict.

Try to not let your buttons be pushed or act out of fear or anger. Simply listen, breathe deeply, and see what's in front of you without rushing in to fix or explain or deny. Know that simply holding a calm, receptive attitude already goes a long way to defusing tension and disagreement. Honor both your feelings and the other party's feelings.

Don't rush to a resolution. If it feels safe to do so, express yourself simply, honestly, and with a degree of vulnerability, and you may inspire the same from the other person. Be on the lookout for trying to solve, to appease, to apologize, to rush in as a savior or scapegoat, or to run away in fear. Talk with the intention of finding common ground and compromise. Be cool and calm, and generously accept apologies or gestures of goodwill after the conflict.

No two conflicts will ever be the same, but as an empath, you can often be pivotal: through an unhealed empath, a disagreement can be amplified many times over, but on the other hand, an empath who is comfortable and emotionally intelligent can set a tone of reconciliation and bring about true healing and peace. It just needs your calm presence and compassion, without fear, judgment, anger, or wanting to control the situation by playing the rescuer, victim, or "good guy."

Most importantly, however, an empath needs to learn to be resilient to conflict that doesn't and cannot be soothed. In a way, some empaths strongly identify with healers and helpers because of their own low threshold for witnessing suffering or discomfort. But can we learn to hold even uncomfortable, unfinished, or difficult emotions?

Luckily, boundaries come in here to help us, too: in doing what we can, we can release the need to work out other people's problems for them, to fix unfixable issues, or pick up the blame in a situation where no one wants to take responsibility. A wise empath knows that sometimes, some things *should* break, and that conflict is a natural part of life that can actually be hindered by well-meaning but misguided attempts to bring everyone into harmony.

You might encounter a situation, group, or person who is not switched on enough emotionally to be able to connect with you or seek resolution. You can have all the compassion in the world for them, and it will not change it: they have made their choice, and you have to make yours. If they are shut down, step away. It's not your work to open them up again.

On the other hand, it may be *you* who feels shut down. If you can feel that your empathy is switched off and you're numb, closed, or hardened, this is your signal to call a timeout. You can follow up the conversation later after you've had some time to digest things. Whatever happens, however, never forget that you are *always* empowered to choose your experience, to allow or disallow certain sensations into your field of awareness, and to decide to act in accordance with your higher values.

When we bear this in mind, the issue of "toxic" people, situations, or things becomes a lot easier to manage. As long as we have our boundaries in place and we are firmly connected to those things that feed and nurture us, it doesn't really matter! As you learn and develop as an empath, you'll get a sense for your own triggers, but in the meantime, it's a good idea to be wary of certain things (note, this doesn't mean to avoid completely, but to show discretion and discernment, and pay close attention to how these things affect you):

- Sensationalistic, fear-mongering, or depressing news, in any form. Human tragedy, war, and injustice are a bigger deal for you than others—be careful about how much of this you allow into your world! It's one thing to be well-informed and knowledgeable, but it's another thing to fall into the rabbit hole of tragedies that you cannot control and that will only affect your mood.

- People who complain chronically at you, without ever intending to help themselves. Those who hold you as a captive audience for their own misery are to be avoided—note, this doesn't mean people are genuinely seeking help, guidance, or support. And yet, still, for those who continue to use you for their own soothing purposes, ask yourself if that is a role you wish to fulfill. Some people just like to air their negativities, and this is a danger zone for you.

- Intense, overly stimulating TV shows, books, events, and music, especially if you also feel you're highly sensitive.

- Selfish, egotistical people who are unable to acknowledge you as a separate person, or value you outside of the care you might provide them. People like this can be a bottomless pit for an empath, and will simply leave when the empath is drained, looking for someone else to fill the gap. Seek relationships with others who also have high empathy, and avoid trying to do someone else's emotional work for them. Call them energy vampires, users, or opportunists—whatever the name, avoid them.

- Unhealthy food, addictive substances, unwholesome urban landscapes, or places where you feel trapped or unwell.

- Sarcastic, mean spirited, apathetic, cynical, or cruel people. The irony is that a wounded empath can be all these things! It's not that negative emotions per se are dangerous and should be avoided (quite the opposite), but rather that an empath's needs and abilities will not be properly appreciated or respected by those who are chronically trapped in these mindsets.

A lot of empaths focus on this last point, getting fixated on the idea of protection and identifying and avoiding people who are "toxic." We need to be careful here. No emotion is "good" or "bad" in itself, and a healthy empath knows how to listen, accept, and be open to whatever their emotional experience is, without judgment or fear.

However, there is a big difference between someone who is experiencing a problem and needs help and support to solve it, and someone who has gotten so used to the negativity that they *don't, won't, or can't help themselves.* This is dangerous for an empath who might not be able to recognize this, and not see that their efforts to cheer up or rescue such a person are doomed to failure. Though an empath might have trouble seeing it, some people cannot be helped by care and empathy alone.

For some people, they have to help *themselves.*

If an empath chooses to spend time around a person who is sapping and draining their energy, it's a loss on two counts: the empath is now exhausted, and the other person is not a single inch closer to being happier. In fact, the situation may be worsened, and they may come to depend on the empath.

Abusive, egotistical, selfish, difficult people may not really share the empath's optimism and striving for healing and wellness—they may just be interested in having a sympathetic audience, or someone to mistreat. Empaths can seldom understand these motivations, but that doesn't mean they don't exist, and that doesn't mean an empath can't be harmed by them.

Here's the irony—empaths, in all their emotional sophistication, can actually be *less* adept at spotting these sorts of people than the average person, because their compassion and desire to help clouds their judgment. By wanting to be the savior, they end up in reality being a magnet for negativity. This negativity can literally weaken an empath's immune system, flood their body with cortisol and inflammation, and exhaust and depress them. Thankfully for you, your body comes with a built-in warning system that always lets you know when you're in the presence of someone who isn't healthy for you—if you listen to it!

There are plenty of clues. Notice if you feel angry, bitter, or incredibly fatigued after an encounter with this person. You may simply not feel like yourself, or have sensations that are a little alien to you, including feeling numb, spacey, or even nauseous.

You may start acting apathetic and even mimicking some negative behavior, like complaining or gossiping. In a general sense, an empath who's been in the company of a "toxic" person without the proper barriers can feel like the life is literally drained from them.

Here, it bears repeating that simply being in a bad mood, being down, or having any negative emotions does not make a person toxic—after all, empaths have down days too! Rather, the toxicity comes in the long-term *pattern* of behavior—it never seems to end no matter what you do.

"Toxic people" are seldom the random strangers you encounter who are rude to you, people you disagree with, or those you have occasional conflicts or awkward moments with. Rather, the kind of relationships that empaths find most toxic are usually long-term relationships—family members or old friends who are kept mostly from a sense of guilt or obligation.

These are the people empaths are likely to get into sometimes lifelong tangles and unconscious contracts with. The game seems to be, "I'll play at fixing you, and you play at being unfixable, and we'll be together forever!"

Empaths can legitimately find themselves snared in relationships like this, but on the other hand, if you routinely seem to encounter toxic people throughout life, it may be a clue that the source of negativity is not really in other people. It may also be a clue that your compassion is blocked or limited because you currently are failing to take care of yourself and your own needs; it can be painful to have these issues reflected back to us in the form of people who make us feel bad. Are they doing it to us, or are we, for our own reasons, *allowing* it?

It can be extremely difficult to set boundaries when it comes to other peoples' pain. How can you not care? And isn't everyone entitled to have support through bad times? Every relationship is bound to have to navigate negative emotions sometime or another, and we'd be awful friends for dropping someone simply because they depended on us on occasion. So how do you decide whether a relationship is really healthy overall, or something you need to move away from?

Here, you need crystal clarity on your own needs and limitations, as well as a practical and realistic outlook. Be as honest as you can and ask yourself these questions:

- On the whole, does the relationship enrich and fulfill me (excluding occasional bad days)?
- Am I with this person out of a sense of shame, guilt, or fear? Is our relationship based on our mutual enjoyment or something else?
- Am I routinely unhappy/unwell/exhausted after spending time with this person?
- Does this person often express a lot of criticism, complaining, emotional dumping, or guilt trip tactics when they're with me?

- Do I feel like I can be my authentic self around this person?
- If I'm honest, what is the real reason I'm staying in this relationship?

The last question can be incredibly empowering because it turns the spotlight from the "toxic" person and onto what the empath can control: their own behavior. There will always be rude, difficult people or simply those we don't get on with. However, if we routinely find ourselves locked into unhealthy dynamics with others, we have to also question our willingness to participate in and maintain such relationships.

Remember that many of the emotional "games" take two to play—they stop the second you become aware of what's happening and do something different.

On Toxic Mismatches

Chat with some empaths, and they will say that all this is well and good, except that there really are bad, exploitative, and dangerous people out there—narcissists or sociopaths who could easily ruin an empath's life. Let's take a closer look at this common pairing, and why narcissists and empaths are so often drawn to one another.

Empaths are compassionate, sensitive, and prone to having weak boundaries, and narcissists are less empathic, unaware of others, and liable to violate others' boundaries to get what they want—a perfect combo.

Narcissists can use empaths to feed their narcissism, but treat them poorly; this the empath forgives because they may be wholly identified with the savior role and never leave. Eventually, the narcissist may "discard" the empath entirely (or any person, for that matter) when they no longer have a use for them, leaving the empath in a terrible state.

It's as though the two extremes of the empathy spectrum unconsciously seek one another out—and the attraction between them is not healthy and genuine, but based on unhealed traumas for both. The narcissist is attractive to the empath because they seem exciting, a little selfish (something the empath has trouble being), in control, perhaps even a lost cause that they can swoop in and rescue. The narcissist is attracted to the empath's weak boundaries, and often loves that the empath will focus all their attention on them, be dependent, forgiving, accommodating, and ultra-supportive to the point of almost disappearing themselves.

The important thing for empaths to realize is that narcissists can present a false identity—they will love an empath as long as they reflect the narcissist's own lofty opinion of themselves, but will discard them the moment the empath realizes the flaws, maybe even blaming the empath.

The empath, often having low self-esteem and confused about their own wants and needs, will often acquiesce to this—a toxic and destructive pairing. The empath keeps thinking that they can solve the problem, win their love, and be happy if only they gave more, sacrificed more, forgave more. The narcissist hungrily eats it up and is not even a little bit satisfied. Manipulation and chaos follow, to the extreme detriment of the empath.

So-called "trauma bonds" can develop, and the relentless push-and-pull even becomes addictive over time. A vicious cycle starts— the empath constantly looks for ways to fix themselves, while the narcissist benefits from an increasingly devoted and obsessed partner.

Luckily, such extreme pairings are avoidable if the empath can do the difficult work of being honest with themselves and going into relationships with open eyes. Red flags include "love bombing" (showering the empath with love early on in a relationship to overwhelm and weaken their defenses), emotional manipulation, gaslighting or that constant gut feeling of always being on edge around this person— commonly confused for love in the early stages of infatuation!

As always, it comes down to boundaries and a sense of self-respect. To listening to that self-preserving gut feeling, and to knowing deep down that you are not on this earth to do anyone else's emotional work for them.

Be cautious of framing yourself as the one who is always responsible for your partner. Don't chase anyone, try to psychologize them, or explain away their behavior, i.e. "He can't help abusing me; he had such a terrible childhood." You don't need to be the brave soul who truly "understands" the misunderstood person.

You don't need to convince them to love you. If the empath can have the presence of mind to put their own wellbeing first, they will not stay in the clutches of an abuser or manipulator for long. How do they do this? By regularly making space for themselves to reflect, integrate, recover, and ground. By constantly refreshing their boundaries. By maintaining strong awareness of their intuition.

Mind games, gaslighting, belittling, withholding affection, silent treatment, sulking, threats and insults, jealousy, possessiveness, lying . . . all of these are what's in store if an empath ignores that quiet voice inside.

It's easy to ignore this voice if you let yourself get carried away in fantasy or "whirlwind" romances that go fast and leave you no time to think or check in with your higher self. Have you unconsciously, one way or another, agreed to the contract, "If I give absolutely everything of myself away, if I violate my own boundaries and do whatever you want, if I suffer enough, will I finally earn your love and be a *good person*?"?

Does your partner reflect back to you your own lack of self-worth? Are you genuinely attracted or merely drawn to someone who can do what you find so difficult—pursue their own self-interest without a second thought? Are your relationships really repeating past traumas and dynamics? Ultimately, how does it serve you to devote yourself to someone else's ego and vanity?

Relationships with narcissists can be devastating for empaths, but they can also be a powerful inflection point in life, and a serious invitation to take better care of ourselves. Sometimes, it takes a brush with a narcissist to truly appreciate what is most wanted in a relationship: an equal who will love and respect you as you do others.

On Partners

The best thing an empath can do before they embark on any romantic relationship is to make sure their relationship with *themselves* is pristine. Unhealthy empaths can become magnets for the very people who can hurt them most, and get stuck in patterns where they are constantly set up as the ones who give and give and give— and never receive. Wanting to heal and care for others is a noble calling, but it can be abused and misdirected, keeping empaths trapped in toxic situations.

An empath's work in this area can be lifelong.

What it usually comes down to is self-worth—knowing that although you can and want to help others, it needn't ever be done at the expense of your wellbeing, and you *never* have to suffer in the hope that it could benefit others somehow. Empaths can have such low self-worth that they attract others who are happy to agree with them!

Likewise an empath can often pre-empt another person's emotions and understand them more deeply than even they can, which can be attractive to those people who are relatively emotionally undeveloped, or else simply want someone else to shoulder their emotional "stuff" while they play victim (or "misunderstood").

In poor relationships, an empath can waste their intuition and sensitivity by directing it solely toward someone else's pathology, when it's far more needed in the empath's own life.

Committed to healing and reconciliation, an empath can forgive what shouldn't be overlooked, make excuses for habits that should rightly be called out, blame themselves when they shouldn't, or assume that every bit of discomfort in their partner is their personal responsibility to fix. Empaths need to use their skills to ground themselves and develop good boundaries, rather than invest their energy into other people's dramas and traumas.

When an empath is in a healthy relationship, they can reach glorious depths of intimacy and love—so don't waste it on someone who cannot appreciate it! When happy and supported, an empath can love with generosity and fearlessness, but with the wrong partner, this can turn into martyrdom and pointless self-sacrifice.

With the wrong partner, an empath can throw themselves away and still feel inadequate, but with someone who respects them, they can soon feel as though their compassion is truly valuable and wanted. Healthy empaths know how to give themselves space; unhealthy ones will periodically blow up and run away from intimacy, then feel guilty for it. Honesty, intuition, intensity—all of these blessings can be curses if they're freely given to a person who cannot appreciate them or reciprocate.

In the early stages of a relationship, an empath can often feel overwhelmed. Your intuition will guide you, but keep a few things in mind:

The right person will always respect how you are right now. They will not make you feel guilty or bad for wanting alone time or space to recuperate and realign.

The right person is someone you feel comfortable being honest with, and will happily communicate with you about *anything*.

The right person will never make you responsible for their emotions, blame you, or expect you to take care of them without returning that care.

The right person makes you feel more like yourself, comfortable, calm, and safe. You will never need to play psychologist, nurse, or savior to an equal, respectful partner.

Empaths can often find themselves lonely despite a deep craving for genuine connection with another. Unable to deal with the complexities of their own emotions, they find engaging with other people extra difficult, not to mention they may feel that the risk of heartbreak is far, far higher than the average person might.

Having permeable boundaries and hypersensitive nervous systems, they can experience romantic relationships as full of angst and drama. For an empath, "merging" completely with a soul mate, becoming one with them and losing oneself, may sound romantic, but is actually unfeasible.

When empaths avoid intimacy or commitment, it's this engulfing version of intimacy they are afraid of. However, if they calibrate to healthy and boundaried levels of engagement, they can develop fulfilling and meaningful relationships just like anyone else can. In existing relationships, empaths can find a lot of relief in keeping things practical: plenty of alone time, proper communication, even separate sleeping arrangements can keep things grounded and realistic.

For single empaths looking for love, the advice is to take it slow. Meditate and journal, perhaps seek therapy and get support from likeminded individuals as you look for the right mate.

As always, trust your own gut. Be aware of any trauma that may have set up attachment styles that don't work for you anymore. Be curious about what you find attractive and why. Many empaths have had to unpick their attraction to narcissistic types and heal low self-esteem and maladaptive beliefs before they could head out into the world and find a person who will love them as they deserve (perhaps even a person who is sensitive and empathic, too?).

What about when romance doesn't work out, as is almost inevitable? The prospect can be almost unbearable for an empath, but a key part of any empath's development is learning to navigate loss. Many empaths have experienced profound loss of love in early childhood, making them extra sensitive to abandonment in adulthood.

An unconscious pattern can emerge: we see ourselves as unlovable and flawed, and if only we do XYZ, then we can win back love again. This traps us in dynamics where our low self-worth is confirmed, and we get stuck trying to "win" back affection, feeling completely devastated if someone leaves us.

It's this compulsion to prove their worth that leads many empaths to be the "wounded healers," codependents, and doormats of the world. The end of a relationship can trigger profound feelings of self-hatred for an empath, who can immediately blame themselves, cling to the partner, or wonder what they did wrong.

It's not hard to see how this pattern can take an empath down the road of abusive, neglectful, imbalanced relationships— precisely the things the empath most wants to escape from early childhood. In the end, heartbreak can teach an empath an immensely difficult lesson: how to have compassion and love *for themselves*.

Breaking harmful relationship patterns takes time, honesty, and gentleness. An empath's first job is not to fix others but turn love and attention to themselves and heal any deep-seated beliefs in their own unworthiness. When they truly understand their value, not only will their relationships be healthier, but they'll be more resilient even in the face of a relationship ending.

A heartbreak is an opportunity to pause, go inside yourself, and do the work—fix boundaries, heal old traumas, and change the harmful stories we tell ourselves about ourselves. Every day, remind yourself that you are worthy of love, that you are fundamentally enough as a person.

Poor relationships can be a mirror and show us what healing we still need to do, reflecting our own unconscious beliefs about ourselves. Empaths are master healers and ultra-compassionate—the trick is to direct all this healing and compassion onto yourself!

Empaths already know how to give; their mission in this life is to learn to *receive*.

If you are hurt, keep your heart open. Ask for healing. Reach out to others for help, and give yourself time. Carefully and kindly release attachments that no longer serve you. Take as much time, space, and rest as you need. Stay in the present, and whatever you do, don't judge the process you're in. Retreat into a little cocoon if you need to, but know you can always emerge later, stronger and more radiant.

On Career

Much of the advice for empath's romantic relationships applies to other areas of their lives, career included. Empaths should seek work that complements rather than undermines their abilities. You're going to be spending at least forty hours a week in a certain type of environment. This is something to be strategic and smart about.

Calm occupations like being an accountant, writer, lawyer, musician, or artist may work, whereas obvious "caring roles" like teacher or nurse can be incredibly draining (despite their appeal!). Empaths have a wide range of personalities and skills, but all will do better in jobs where feelings and emotions are acknowledged and respected. Low-intensity work often appeals, as do smaller groups, routine, structure, and a degree of independence to self-direct.

What ultimately works for an empath may be a matter of degree: social work or counseling may be wonderful part time, but hellish if the empath feels rushed, overburdened, or unable to make a real impact. The focus is on the emotional depth and ability, and how it is respected and appreciated.

Empaths can feel worn down by excessive bureaucracy, ultra-fast paced or competitive work environments, falseness, "politics," or having to encounter angry, sick, or scared people regularly. Even sales jobs can be difficult because there is no down time, and your ultimate goal of making a sale will supersede any emotional boundaries you might wish to draw.

They seldom thrive in sales, PR, politics, advertising, or cut-throat or unethical corporate environments. Working from home, working alone, virtual work, and self-employment are often preferred—empaths need the liberty to be able to step back when necessary and make their own hours. Remember, we wish to optimize for the ability to self-protect and draw boundaries, and not every type of work allows for this. Anything unpredictable can undercut this freedom to self-care.

Strong, healthy empaths can take on more challenging work because they know how to manage the stress of others and have firm boundaries and great self-care routines. On the other hand, a wounded empath can have difficulty with *any* occupation, no matter how perfect it seems on paper. This is why it's necessary for empaths to do an honest inventory of not only their strengths and weaknesses, but also their own unique set of preferences. Are they more or less introverted?

Do they like structured or open-ended work? Flexibility makes all the difference— you may not be able to handle being a teacher, but if you really love children, you can find fulfilling work in being a children's librarian or author of kid's books, for example.

Even the perfect occupation will come with some work pressure, and so empaths of all kinds will need to develop coping skills. Occasional tough work situations are just part of life—but an empath can manage them by consciously choosing not to take on the negative emotions of others and regularly giving themselves time to decompress, ground, and recharge.

Take breaks throughout the day or after a conflict to breathe and recalibrate. Take time to acknowledge and name your feelings, and unpick what's yours and what isn't. Sink into your body to just let yourself become aware of your gut intuition. Then ask: what thoughts, emotions, and actions will serve me right now?

Taking the time to do this will allow you to take conscious control of your own emotional experience and get the result you want. Use a spirit of gratitude, acceptance, and compassion to open up to what your intuition is telling you to do next. Your high emotional intelligence is a real asset at work if you take the time to apply it wisely!

Without becoming cynical about it, understand that workplace rules are not the same rules that you live your own life by— they do *not* make room for emotions. It may seem obvious, but empaths need to remind themselves that others are not like them, and will not always be kind, so you shouldn't expect it.

Empaths need to understand that not everyone is worth their kindness, either, and that many people will not need, want, or even understand their help. Other people may be on different wavelengths—they don't feel what you do and don't want to. And that's okay! A smart empath sees this, accepts it, and takes steps to maximize their own happiness given these workplace truths. At work, you may need firmer boundaries, a little more control, and more objectivity.

On the other hand, your intuition will tell you when a work environment is truly unsustainable, and you should simply leave. If this is the case, leave. Without second-guessing yourself. Trust that you will find a better place to make use of your skills. The worst-case scenario is that you will end up in the same or similar job.

There is no real justification for feeling dread and anxiety for something you will be spending most of your waking hours doing. It's a recipe for disaster and lack of fulfillment; a dry and subtle feeling that something is wrong, without the ability to rectify it.

Takeaways

- The empath can't keep putting up defenses and blocks to the loud and noisy world; he or she must simply learn to operate better within it. First, the empath can improve at defending needs and desires. This consists of being extremely clear on what is desired, and being intentional about it.

- Observe your emotions and try to not be affected or overwhelmed by them. Observe them and watch them pass you by like waves crashing on the beach. The world will never be less noisy, but you can deal with it a little bit better.

- Resolve conflict by drawing boundaries and learning to say no. This is not easy and in fact is intensely uncomfortable for most, even non-empaths. But remember what is at stake for you. It's not just an hour of your time, or a bit of money—it's about your emotional state that must be cared for and cultivated. Closely related to this is to understand your actions, and if you are doing it for you or someone else covertly.

- Avoid negative people and even news sources. This is completely within your control, and it removes a source of instant anxiety. In a similar vein, stop going out of your way to help and assist people. You might not realize it presently, but this is also another source of stress and pressure that is unnecessary and even unhealthy. All of these elements in this chapter can be present in your intimate relationships and career—or not. Now that we have a solid understanding and framework for what plays well with the particularities of the empath, a clear path should emerge for partners and career paths: time to recharge, emotionally even-keeled and stable, understanding and nurturing environments, not high pressure, working with people (but not to the point of overwhelm), and so on.

Chapter Five. How to Handle with Care

Thus far, we've discussed a wide range of how you, the empath, can navigate the world more effectively. But what about when you come into contact with someone? It's not as easy as imagining that an empath is just like you, and acting the same.

An empath is a brilliant friend to have—just as you likely are. They're generous, understanding, and can inspire and heal those around them—what's not to love? Enjoy this type of deep emotional support, because it can bring feelings of great satisfaction, validation, and intimacy.

However, if you're friends with an empath or want to be, it's worth remembering your/their vulnerabilities, too.

Empaths are sensitive and switched on—they'll just *know* things. You might see them constantly stand up for the underdog or look for the good in everyone. They're super tolerant of everyone's differences but can be perceived as shy and aloof, even though this is more likely just introversion and being a little bit fatigued.

If you're friends with an empath, be aware that they may not always be able to be as sociable as you'd like, and may have to cancel plans occasionally, leave events early, or call time-out while they retreat for some alone time. This is not a reflection on you or your relationship!

If an empath does seem flaky and non-committal, try to remember that deep down, they do crave connection, but they have often been hurt before and are merely doing what they can to manage the intensity of their emotions and avoid conflict or overwhelm.

You'll win their love by respecting their need to do this without questioning it or making them feel bad. If you can give them space, an empath can easily become one of your closest friends. Avoid gossip, complaining, or unconsciously using them as therapists—the empath will always bend over backward for you, but that doesn't mean you should abuse this privilege. Make a point of encouraging them to ask for help, support them, be loyal to them and respect who they are, without wanting to change them.

In friendship, an empath wants an equal, a kindred spirit who isn't afraid to open their heart wide. They know how to give, and they want the same in return.

It's true that they can sometimes be preachy or controlling—but they usually just want to help. Be kind, authentic, and open-minded, and an empath will soon trust and respect you. The fastest way to lose that respect is by demanding too much of them, violating their boundaries, judging them, or being overly harsh—save the aggressive "jokes" and playful insults for other friends. Empaths hate conflict and drama—if you have an issue with them, they'll always appreciate it if you can talk to them honestly, focusing on feelings. If you do so, you'll always find a friend quick to forgive and move on.

And what about the next step—a romantic relationship with an empath?

The first step is to be a good friend to them! Being in a romantic relationship with an empath may be the most intense, fulfilling, and profound experience of your life, but it's not without considerable challenges. If you're interested in, dating, or even already in a relationship with an empath, understanding and respecting who they are will be at the core of your relationship's success.

Empaths can live in a world that seems too intense to other people; they love deeply, and it gets complicated fast, with the empath frequently bringing past trauma to the table.

The key is to have trust and compassion, and to go slow. The biggest practical issue to bear in mind is that these "emotional sponges" will need plenty of alone time to recharge. It's a mistake to take this personally, to insist that you spend every moment together, or to make them feel guilty. Whatever you do, don't impose emotional problems on an empath or take advantage of their helping instincts—they'll help you, but to their and your detriment.

Make sure you clearly negotiate social schedules, alone time needs, and even sleeping and domestic arrangements. Ask, don't demand, and *never* yell or show violence.

Empaths need partners who can go beneath superficialities—often very deep beneath them. They may not be social butterflies, and can sometimes experience extremely low moods. Give them time to sort it out for themselves, and offer kind, nonjudgmental support without rushing them.

You may sometimes wonder if you're an empath's "fix up" project, as though they'd like to rescue or save you—here, you need clear boundaries to help the empath identify when they're falling into this parenting/savior role. Always be calm, self-sufficient, and responsible for your own emotions. This frees the empath to work on their own "stuff"!

Empaths can sometimes take life and themselves very seriously—so your best approach is often a lighthearted one. Be playful and remind them to connect to the moment, to their bodies. Make them laugh. Be authentic and honest—empaths can never connect with a liar or someone who presents a false front.

As long as you make time to communicate often and from the heart, a relationship with an empath can be deeply rewarding. But try to control an empath, change who they are, guilt-trip them, rush them, mock them, or doubt their intuition, and you may create a rift that's hard to fix.

With all this in mind, an empath doesn't need pity, protection, or to be treated as a delicate flower. Don't make excuses for them or imply that they're mentally ill, "too much," or overreacting. Finally, sometimes the kindest thing you can do for an empath is to leave if things truly aren't going well. The trouble is that an empath will often hold on to a failing relationship long after they should. Know when to step away in kindness. It will hurt, but it will hurt less if done with honesty and compassion.

The final aspect of handling with care is how to navigate empaths in a family unit, and more specifically, as a parent or caregiver.

Empaths typically show their abilities from a very young age—how do you know if your child is an empath? A keen-eyed parent will be able to sense when a child is overstimulated—by sounds, smells, busyness, loud TV, rushed schedules, strong emotions, or conflict. These are children who can be misdiagnosed with a range of disorders, or simply described as "shy." A thoughtful, quiet, sensitive child, however, needs their parents' understanding and support more than anything. In fact, they need one hundred percent unconditional love as they learn how to be themselves in a world that won't quite understand them.

Wanting to escape social situations, responding strongly to stories or TV, showing deep compassion to others and animals, needing lots of alone time, having only a few close friends rather than a crowd, and getting upset by others' pain are some signs to watch out for. These are the children who will pick up on the subtlest emotional shifts in the household and can often be deeply anxious. As their parent, it's up to you to model grounding behavior that they can eventually learn as self-care when they are adults.

Don't overschedule or rush—let your child embrace the present, and encourage awareness of movement and their bodies. Teach them early on to recognize and name emotions, and let them know that whatever these are, *they will pass.* Making clear that emotions are normal and deserve to be acknowledged is important so they don't begin to think that something is wrong with themselves.

Encourage young empaths to understand early on where their boundaries are, and empower them to know that they can say no—you teach them this by respecting the boundaries they put up for you! A young empath will always respond well to heart-centered communication. Encourage meditative activities and plenty of outdoor time. Give them space and the tools they need to be creative. Cultivate a home free of emotional drama and conflict.

You don't want to wrap your child in cotton wool to protect them forever, and you certainly don't want to communicate to them that they are somehow weak, fragile, or damaged for being different—rather, teach them the skills that will most encourage wellbeing in their adulthood: the ability to set firm boundaries and a deep, unshakeable belief in their own self-worth.

Takeaways

- This last chapter is a brief look at how other people might function around you, and thus, allow you to take a look at other empaths. Even though you might internalize many of these actions for yourself, you may not have the experience of dealing with other empaths. So let's take a quick look at how to handle with care, just as you prefer to be handled.
- Give them space and be tolerant of their limits. Don't be pushy when you sense something might be against their wishes

or intentions; they may want to satisfy and please you, but that can ultimately be too self-sacrificing.

- Understand their drive to help, feel, relate, and validate. But don't take advantage of it, and make sure that they are doing exactly what they want, without trying to accommodate you.

- Give them space. This needs to be repeated, but in an emotional manner. Try to not make it a habit to constantly unload your negative emotions on them. Remember that empaths are emotional sponges and will soak up everything around them—don't be the one who will bring them down.

- Finally, just be kind. Almost everything the empath wants is geared toward a positive outcome, something kind in return to you. So give them the benefit of the doubt.

Summary Guide

Chapter One. Diagnosing the Empath

- What is an empath? Are you one? Why does the world appear so differently to you than to your friends? What is the cause of this, and what exactly is going on? You may very well be an empath. An empath is a person with a heightened capacity for empathy, or someone with the ability to feel the emotions of others.
- You feel *deeply*, and it's not a choice. Rather than merely understanding another person's state of mind on an *intellectual* level, empaths seem to "let more in, and can find themselves literally feeling the emotional reality of another person. We can understand empaths as supremely *emotionally intelligent* in the way that some people are gifted with musical ability or are born with heightened taste buds and become acclaimed chefs.

- There are several models and theories that try to understand the development of the empathic personality, but most of them fall in roughly four categories: genetics (i.e. empaths inherit the trait from their parents as a result of literally different brain chemistry in the form of mirror neurons and/or emotional contagion sensitivity), temperament or character (usually as a coping mechanism for self-protection, combined with a hazy understanding of personal boundaries), the result of childhood trauma (which for an empath can be something surprising) or, on the other hand, the result of positive parenting that helps those with inborn gifts to develop them properly.
- Most empaths feel that their unique blend of characteristics is both a blessing and a drawback; a gift and a curse. On some days, they may feel proud of their totally different, often beautiful and rich perspective on the world, and on other days, it can feel like a burden and something to carefully manage in a world that doesn't properly

cater to them. It really comes down to awareness and harnessing this ability rather than letting it run roughshod all over your life.

- There is simply no area of life where increased emotional awareness, respect for others, and a heightened capacity for awareness are not advantageous. But an empath who isn't given the time to recuperate, integrate, and heal themselves can even hurt others, become depressed or anxious, or feel generally crazy.

Chapter Two. Defining and Differentiating

- What is the difference between empaths and what could be called an intense sense of empathy? In truth, they are highly related. They both involve the ability to place themselves in other people's shoes and experience the emotions along with them. They feel deeply and are sometimes unable to avoid being affected. It is not something that they must consciously summon; they are immersed in it, and it is the primary way in which they relate to the world and people. There can be said to be a few different types of empathy: cognitive, emotional, somatic, compassion, and spiritual.

- As we understand more about the human mind and how not everyone fits into a box, we have expanded definitions for what normal can be. It's important to distinguish between other new, expanded definitions to better understand what drives the empath. To be clear, there can be significant overlaps between these personality classifications, but there are also significant overlaps between the summer months and ice cream consumption. It doesn't always mean much. Highly Sensitive People are empaths without the focus on emotional energy, introverts prefer to spend more time alone, and codependents are empaths but with a savior complex and a lack of personal boundaries.

- Then we come to the narcissists, who can be said to be the polar opposite of empaths. Whereas the narcissist has too little, the empath has too much. Unfortunately, there is a special kind of chemistry between these two personality classifications that make them fit together in a fatal way.

Chapter Three. Self-Awareness, Self-Protection, and Self-Care

- Healthy empaths need to prioritize their own personal wellbeing and development, and they need to frame and nurture their gifts in a way that is meaningful and empowering for *them*. A common idea is to use your gifts with discernment, and to realize that you can empathize at will, *or choose not to.* Empaths learn true self-worth and agency by knowing when and how to draw the lines between self and other. This all points to one important concept in personal relationships: boundaries.

- Empaths can very easily feel downright responsible for the feelings and wellbeing of the people around them. But this is a boundary-less mindset, and it makes you a servant to the people around you, while ignoring your own needs. It is necessary to self-prioritize.

- Empaths also need to be cognizant of their energy and fatigue levels. Both of these can easily lead to a level of overwhelm that can be incapacitating. And for what, a lack of self-awareness? This is a tactic of self-protection, just like making sure that you have enough gas in your car's tank. Not only do empaths have to worry about normal fatigue, but also absorbing emotion and stress from others, and even compassion fatigue. This can all be accomplished with a growing comfort with saying no, strategic scheduling, and simply knowing your needs.

- Finally, empaths must be especially careful that their actions are not influenced by past traumas. Things are magnified, and for our purposes, we should broaden the definition of trauma to those *past experiences that subconsciously make us react in strong ways against our intentions*. Most often these things put us into a state of heightened arousal that is not pleasant to constantly experience, and adds to overwhelm and anxiety.

Chapter Four. Empath Survival Tactics

- The empath can't keep putting up defenses and blocks to the loud and noisy world; he or she must simply learn to operate better within it. First, the empath can improve at defending needs and desires. This consists of being extremely clear on what is desired, and being intentional about it.

- Observe your emotions and try to not be affected or overwhelmed by them. Observe them and watch them pass you by like waves crashing on the beach. The world will never be less noisy, but you can deal with it a little bit better.

- Resolve conflict by drawing boundaries and learning to say no. This is not easy and in fact is intensely uncomfortable for most, even non-empaths. But remember what is at stake for you. It's not just an hour of your time, or a bit of money—it's about your emotional state that must be cared for and cultivated. Closely related to this is to understand your actions, and if you are doing it for you or someone else covertly.

- Avoid negative people and even news sources. This is completely within your control, and it removes a source of instant anxiety. In a similar vein, stop going out of your way to help and assist people. You might not realize it presently, but this is also another source of stress and pressure that is unnecessary and even unhealthy. All of these elements in this chapter can be present in your intimate relationships and career—or not. Now that we have a solid understanding and framework for what plays well with the particularities of the empath, a clear path should emerge for partners and career paths: time to recharge, emotionally even-keeled and stable, understanding and nurturing environments, not high pressure, working with people (but not to the point of overwhelm), and so on.

Chapter Five. How to Handle with Care

- This last chapter is a brief look at how other people might function around you, and thus, allow you to take a look at other empaths. Even though you might internalize many of these actions for yourself, you may not have the experience of dealing with other empaths. So let's take a quick look at how to handle with care, just as you prefer to be handled.
- Give them space and be tolerant of their limits. Don't be pushy when you sense something might be against their wishes or intentions; they may want to satisfy and please you, but that can ultimately be too self-sacrificing.
- Understand their drive to help, feel, relate, and validate. But don't take advantage of it, and make sure that they are doing exactly what they want, without trying to accommodate you.
- Give them space. This needs to be repeated, but in an emotional manner.

Try to not make it a habit to constantly unload your negative emotions on them. Remember that empaths are emotional sponges and will soak up everything around them—don't be the one who will bring them down.

- Finally, just be kind. Almost everything the empath wants is geared toward a positive outcome, something kind in return to you. So give them the benefit of the doubt.

CPSIA information can be obtained
at www.ICGtesting.com
Printed in the USA
LVHW051526170723
752377LV00003B/123